Encounters with Living Language...

"This clear wise book about renewing our connection with sacred language will bring all who read it benefit and inspiration."
—**Andrew Harvey**
Author of *The Hope* and *Engoldenment*

"This consciousness-expanding title digs into flashes of profound insight that might strike one while reading, those moments of revelatory connection to language and, perhaps, something else beyond it, such as the very 'source from which words rise and return.'...Seekers and transcendent-minded readers will find Donnell's accounts fascinating, and her example of growing with each 'illumination' heartening."
—*Booklife Reviews*

"An exceptional glimpse into the fascinating connections between language and the hidden depths of human consciousness."
—**Beatrice Toothman**
Manhattan Book Review

"Christina Donnell is a seer. When I read her first book, *Transcendent Dreaming*, I was impressed by the depth of her wisdom, grounded in both mystical and practical experience. I now consider her among the conduits used by some higher source of wisdom to convey teachings to humanity. In *Encounters with Living Language*, she offers fascinating glimpses at what it is like to live guided by deep, prophetic insight."

—Rick Archer
Creator and host of Buddha at the Gas Pump

"Here Christina Donnell introduces a new possibility for humanity: a transcendent experience with the potential to dissolve the myth of separation that alienates us from our original goodness. It presences a numinous intelligence through the light emanating from her narrative and stories. This book must be read with the whole body and all the senses."

—Michael Stone
Host of The Shift Network's
Shamanic Wisdom Summit and WE Earth Radio

"As wisdom teachings tell us, and as chronicled so beautifully in *Encounters with Living Language*, words have not only meaning but an intrinsic power of revelation.... As wonderfully shared in Donnell's book, our words that seek to imbue our lives with meaning inevitably reflect and illuminate the deeper, ineffable truth of the whole world."

—Jude Currivan, PhD
Cosmologist, author, and
cofounder of WholeWorld-View

"A beautifully written book. Readers will walk away thinking about how language affects them in their daily lives."

—Kyle Eaton
San Francisco Book Review

"Christina Donnell's book is illuminating and uplifting. Her powerful intimate stories bring energy to language and language to life. Her profound yet obtainable teachings, free of spiritual dogma, inspire us to look deeper and realize what is possible."

—Tim Rumsey, MD
Founding physician of United Family Practice
and author of *Pictures from a Trip*

"A mind-blowing exploration of the potential role language could play. This book will trigger transformative thoughts and an increased level of awareness."

—**Foluso Falaye**
Seattle Book Review

"Between the words of this book there is an energy that flows around us and stirs the consciousness, enkindling a journey in which creation is given voice and original ground is revealed within. All of creation is calling for us to awaken! Thank you, Christina, for illuminating the path."

—**Jyoti Ma**
Founder of The Fountain for the Natural Order of Our Existence

"Opening to language in this way, we find a tool that touches our evolution. This book isn't just another idea; it is a living transmission."

—**Mary Jo Peppler**
International Volleyball Hall of Fame and two-time Olympian

Encounters with Living Language

Also by Christina Donnell, PhD

Transcendent Dreaming:
Stepping into Our Human Potential

ENCOUNTERS
with
LIVING
LANGUAGE

Surrendering to the Power of Words

Christina Donnell, PhD

Winds of Change Books
Saint Paul, Minnesota

Published by: Winds of Change Books
2388 University Avenue West
Saint Paul, MN 55114
www.windsofchangebooks.com

Editor: Ellen Kleiner
Book design and production: Janice St. Marie

FIRST EDITION

Encounters with Living Language is factually accurate, except
that names, locales, and individual traits have been altered to
preserve coherence while protecting privacy.

Printed in Canada

Publisher's Cataloging-in-Publication Data
Names: Donnell, Christina, author.
Title: Encounters with living language : surrendering to the
power of words / Christina Donnell.
Description: First edition. | St. Paul, Minnesota :
Winds of Change Books, [2023]
Identifiers: ISBN: 978-0-9801810-0-5 (Paperback) | 978-0-
9801810-1-2 (eBook) | LCCN: 2022917613
Subjects: LCSH: Psycholinguistics. | Metalanguage. | Enlight-
enment. | Creativity (Linguistics) | Language and
emotions. | Meaning (Psychology) | Awareness. | Per-
ception. | Mind and body. | Interoception. | Self-con-
sciousness (Awareness) | Senses and sensation. |
Self-actualization (Psychology) | BISAC: BODY,
MIND & SPIRIT / Inspiration & Personal Growth.
Classification: LCC: BF458 .D66 2023 | DDC: 401/.9--dc23

1 3 5 7 9 10 8 6 4 2

To Santi, Miguel,
and the stewards of tomorrow

Contents

Introduction

Between 1997 and 2015, I experienced ninety-two illuminations on language and its deeper function in human awakening, each a consciousness-expanding moment inspired by a message from the invisible world. I call these moments illuminations because they "light up" from within, an effect seemingly born of the body's native capacity to resonate with other bodies and the environment, and simultaneously propel a marked shift toward higher consciousness.

I clearly remember the mystifying day in 1997 when a new form of consciousness first arose in me occasioned by an encounter with language. The event changed my life like an evolutionary mutation in a species, akin, perhaps, to how pterosaur's inaugural flight disrupted its reptilian perspective or how the advent of higher order thinking unsettled the world of *Homo erectus,* suddenly rendering jobless many faculties kept gainfully employed for years.

Not until 2012 did I experience a second illumination, followed by ninety others by 2015. Over those three years, the messages seemed increasingly urgent, as if delivery of their content were intrinsic to a progressively expanding trajectory of human consciousness. Also, they all had to do with language, which I found puzzling. During many illuminations, it was as if I became one with language, feeling its rhythm in my somatic-sensory system and my body as part of its composition. During others, the silences between words provided clues to their messages. As the illuminations kept coming, I began to think that accepting them might prepare me to become a conduit through which language's expanded function for the future might be imparted.

Within twenty-four hours of the occurrence of each illumination, I emailed a description of its content to my editor, who graciously archived these writings. I never looked at them again until recently, because I could not easily understand their content with my conscious mind. Upon retrieving them some months ago, I saw that the illuminations, which revealed their significance solely through somatic-sensory receptors below the level of consciousness, were leading me to experience the source from which words rise and return, resulting in a progressive attunement with the greater universe. Because of the potentially wide-ranging applications of this startling discovery, I felt it important to share a sampling of the illuminations, more than a dozen of which appear in the pages that follow.

The chapters, arranged chronologically, detail the moments surrounding these illuminations, as well as their impact on me. There was a certain uniformity to their delivery: they penetrated my consciousness when thought was suspended; they conveyed fresh truths from beyond with startling abruptness, conferring a direct knowing in the form of clairvoyant intuitions or prophetic hints; all the while there was a passage from one plane to another, during which I received the transmissions with such intensity that their messages carried more conviction than those ordinarily perceived. Less predictable, and often radically variable, were their effects on my awareness—leading me to see that even the power of a word, including the intervals before and after it, depends on the state of the recipient and of the source from which the word originates. I have since come to realize that a person attuned to the silence from which a word emerges and returns becomes a radio receiver through which the voice of the universe is transmitted.

Each chapter opens in the present tense, primarily to recapture the immediacy of the illuminations, ground their rarefied nature, and intimately document the circumstances that prepared me to receive them. By echoing in real time the original events, their retelling re-creates for the reader the states of emptiness, silence, stillness, non-doing, and presence that seemed integral to the progressive unfolding of awareness I experienced following each illumination. It was through such states that my encounters with language awakened me to realities beyond the everyday world, where conceptual thought gives way to direct knowing—an immersion into what I have since come to call "living language."

Encounters with Living Language is for anyone who has heard or read a poignant line and, when penetrated by its meaning, had chills or felt the hairs rising on the back of their neck. It is also for anyone who has experienced the luminous power of language and, as a result, felt compelled to explore its quantum nature ushering in new dimensions of awareness. The book not only reflects the corridors of this journey but reveals the role language could play in the profound changes currently occurring in human consciousness. It does so by taking the reader through an internal experience of language in which expanded states of awareness emerge. Its ultimate aim is to renew our human bearings, to prompt recollection and reestablishment of the rootedness of human awareness in the surrounding ecosystem.

Due to its timeliness, this book is also for anyone interested in simply entering into a more profound relationship with language. No prior experience is needed. After all, a deeper immersion in the hidden potential of language—well beyond its use to convey surface meanings—may not only help elevate our awareness but possibly move us along an evolutionary trajectory. In fact, such a transition may have already begun. Amidst the old use of language, representing physical realities, still governing ordinary consciousness, new, expanded functions may be emerging so modestly and unintrusive as to be imperceptible to most people while having a heightening effect on their consciousness. The enduring beauty of human awakening occurring through a deeper interaction with language is its universality: it is a process free of spiritual dogma. I offer my chronicles of surrendering to the power of words as inspiration for others to explore the immeasurable potential of language, which exists in each of us.

1

Experiencing a Privileged Moment with Language

During privileged moments, sensations are heightened; the motion of spoken words conveys a sense of boundlessness; the pulse of time dissolves into waves of eternity.

IT IS LATE SUMMER 1997, and I am in the Montana mountains with my friend Mary Ellen as she performs a funeral rite for her partner, a Lakota medicine man who recently passed. Days go by, time drops away, and we enter a place between worlds. Inside her tent, Mary Ellen sings low, throaty songs in the old language that sound like the wind. The spell of wilderness makes me feel unified with the landscape, immersed in a world of brown tangled-together growing things. Late summer bustles with buckskin seedpods, and silver filaments fly into warm air, urgently seeking a resting place to grow. Lichens breathe on rocks, along with yellow-green mosses, soft as clouds. Swallows dip and circle, and dragonflies shoot past, as if all the amorous activity of late summer is woven weblike together. I'm grasped by rhythms of life flowing in deeper levels of the self. Even the passing of a friend seems intrinsic to this flow.

When Mary Ellen completes her ceremony, we make our way to the closest small town. We are full, floating in silence, wearing the face of the Montana sky. Upon arrival, we enter a diner in hopes of finding a hot meal. Here we catch up on the news of the week, which includes the deaths of Princess Diana and Mother Teresa.

After vegetable stew and coffee, I leave Mary Ellen tinkering with her old Honda Accord, which will not start, and walk leisurely through the town. I come upon a small church with signage that announces a mass to celebrate Mother Teresa's life commencing in fifteen minutes. Although it has been decades since I have been in a house of worship, suddenly I feel compelled to pay my respects to Mother Teresa.

I sit quietly in the back row of the church, enjoying a subdued bliss moving through me. Midway through the service an invisible wave of something like dread undulates over my flesh, causing me chills from head to toe, as if enveloped in a breaker's crest, where it froths and whitens.

Standing behind the simple wood altar, the priest retreats into himself, his prayer losing its leaves and drooping out of his mouth like a withered shrub. The young altar boys come back from the platform withdrawn, as though turned inside out. A dead silence reigns in the room.

After the service, I slip quickly outside and walk to a nearby imposing oak tree. On the other side of the tree sits one of the young altar boys, with his back against it, hands clasped around one raised knee, face turned down and toward the street. In its direction, he says, "I liked Mother Teresa's kindness." After a long pause, without looking up, he asks, "What did you like about her?"

Feeling a strange urgency, under the influence of the smoothing movement of his hand around his knee or his fair, drooping hair I advance a few steps in the direction of his stare and bend down to gaze into his eyes. At first he continues to look into the distance, but when his eyes finally meet mine I experience a state of resonance, like something singing me.

I hear myself say: "What I admired most was her courage to stand up for what is…not…right." I am surprised by my comment because it doesn't really express what I admired most about Mother Teresa. I become immediately aware of how the spaces around words begin losing their struts and fibers, their structural forces that aid comprehension. And I note how my emphasis on the words *is not right* seems jarring when used in connection with the words *stand up for*, a usage that challenges syntax and coherence.

The boy, too, seems momentarily transfixed, perhaps experiencing the same unspoken resonance. The space between us becomes dehiscent, as if dandelion pollen is being released in the wind. In a flash, I see the boy telling his mother how the priest exploited him sexually, and somehow know that he will do this soon. I also know many Catholic priests will be implicated in child sexual abuse in years to come.

I shudder in silence. The boy's posture reflects discomfort, and he rises but remains silent, perhaps enduring ghostlike personal terrors. We stand there stiffly, seized by the moment until his parents approach, breaking the silence with their voices. I walk away from the encounter trembling, as if having absorbed the exploits I envisioned.

The circumstances revealed to me that day twenty-five years ago were ultimately confirmed. Several months later reports of the priest's sexual exploitation of young parish boys hit the news. The parents of the boy I encountered were one of three couples interviewed when the story went public. Subsquently, the Catholic Church faced multiple lawsuits for sexual abuse by parish priests worldwide.

What I sensed at the time had been a presentiment of the future. Never before did I imagine that such expanded awareness could result from unspoken resonances attending spoken words. What surprised me about the exchange with the boy was not the prophetic revelation, since I'd had a long history of receiving such knowledge and had come to think I was simply a passing womb for invisible forces desiring to emerge into the world. The revelation for me was the role of language, how the unusual usage of a phrase and spaces between words within it suggested a larger meaning. It taught me that a moment in dialogue can become detached from those around it and open to unspoken truths unfettered by time, causing past, present, and future to occur simultaneously in an instant.

Such moments stand out, and their effects last. In them, a special kind of silence heightens sensibilities and makes meaning more profound. I've come to call them "privileged moments," since during the emergence of such concentrated and luminous language there is mystery and, despite our limited understanding of its meaning, immediate comprehension. During privileged moments, sensations are heightened; the motion of spoken words conveys a sense of boundlessness; the pulse of time dissolves into waves of eternity; and the notion of being a separate self participating in the external world disappears, culminating in awareness beyond everyday perception.

My privileged moment with the boy at church impacted the innermost part of my being, where latent faculties arise as fragile beginnings. I came to regard it as expressive of an evolution in human consciousness, or at least a perceptual modification allowing for a new form of awareness. I determined that it had been catalyzed by my encounter with living language arising from invisible forces residing in the spoken word's border with the senses. Fifteen years would pass before I'd again experience a somatic-sensory impression enkindling comprehension in an unexpected and profound way, followed by countless more such events.

2

Language's Mouthpiece

It is time to do what you were born to do.
Be language's mouthpiece.

I HEAR THE VOICE OF MY great-grandmother Maggie floating toward me through an open window like a soft breeze. "The wind is never weary," I whisper to her while my body grows leaden. My friend Rosa holds me tightly as though to keep me in the world, but everything is fading fast. I am being sucked into a tunnel of mist, my soul wafting up through the passage where darkness and light swirl in an endless vortex. I feel with a certainty close to divination that I am to die of yellow fever here in the high Andes of Peru on this fine late winter morning, with my mission to secure parental guidance for my godson Miguel incomplete.

Then the dimness fades from my eyes to reveal the face of Santi, my soul friend and lover whom I know to be dead, having been struck by lightning three months earlier. He comes forward to embrace me, tenderly strokes my hair, and over my fevered body chants the intonations he used to hum when I lay awake at night. He then gently pushes me away from him, and, no longer floating upward, I am crashing down like a deer breaking through ice, tumbling to a pond's bedrock. Something is propelling me back through the tunnel, out of the realm of spirit into the world of flesh and blood.

Everything dims into nothingness except for a needle-sharp pain piercing my temples like a dagger that will not stop stabbing, leaving me in such agony that I fear my skull will explode. Soon a brilliant light appears, wrenching me from my stupor. The light sears me, my bones floating up like a dream rising to the top of sleep. All I can do is gape at the overpowering brilliance. Then from that luminosity comes a voice that shakes me to my core, reverberating in my heart as it commands: "I am the original light that illuminates the living word. It is time to do what you were born to do. Be language's mouthpiece."

The puzzling command seems to call for a mission with urgency but no clues for implementing it, making it at once mandatory yet mysterious. The light dazzles every cell in my body as I thrash in its grip, trying to absorb more of its message. I pant with fever while Rosa and others gather around, powerless to ease my agony.

Seven days pass, and I do not die. Instead, I rally, sitting up to sip a broth of sweet, steamed *yaron* soaked in alpaca milk that Rosa offers me. Verdant powers stir quietly inside me as I begin to live again. Imperceptible delicate waves of energy keep coming in, as though my soul has been given ears to hear what the mind does not understand.

On the ninth day of my ordeal, Santi's longtime friend Simone walks into the hut, bringing with him the aroma of horse sweat mingled with alpaca blanket wool. I stand, with Rosa and her husband steadying my weakened body. Simone greets me with smiling eyes, not uttering a word, and the four of us step into the fresh air. He hoists me into a horse's saddle, easing my feet into the stirrups, and although he speaks Quechua he says in Spanish, "*Estás firme y silenciosa para montar. Solo tienes que*

sentarte en la silla y confiar en él para que te lleve.
(You are steady and quiet to ride. You have only
to sit in the saddle and trust him to carry you.)"
Simone then leads my horse down the mountain to
Cusco, where a plane is waiting to take me back to
the United States.

I have narrowly escaped death by yellow fever,
and my near-death experience seems to have activated some secret ether in my body that makes me
feel light like a bird. Having survived my ordeal, I
resolve to take on the challenge of becoming language's mouthpiece by openly acknowledging the
power of words.

3

The Energy of Living Language

Language seems to liberate within me
an alluring pull into life and consequently
is intensely enlivening while giving glimpses
of the interconnectedness of all things.

NOW, DURING MY CONVALESCENCE from yellow fever
back home in Minneapolis, I still struggle with
headaches, fainting, and, when tired, cognitive
deficits related to spelling and comprehension. This
summer of illness bares the bitter fruit of loss. With
Santi's death, my heart is turned upside down. Living a thousand years will not make me forget the
days and nights we spent together. It is said that
absence conquers, but his absence vanquishes me.
I feel desireless. The husk of my outer and inner life
falls into slow, compostable decay.

ENCOUNTERS WITH LIVING LANGUAGE

I know that one way of living has come to completion for me. I experience a growing emptiness. Although I have meditated for twenty-five years, I have not sought emptiness; it has been bestowed upon me, along with an unearthly stillness. I realize the emptiness is not a vacuum but rather energy without a center, so that what comes from within it—the eternal—may be incarnated through me in time. I am well aware that from the impression of emptiness there springs a vast amount of energy. This is how I heal.

One night three weeks after my return from Peru a deep sleep comes over me, I float down and am held in darkness, like an animal in quicksand, by something I can't escape. Suddenly, out of the darkness an unnatural light floods my entire body, and I feel a pulse quicken in my temples. Then, in a dream state, I awaken in an underground tunnel dimly lit by two candles, surrounded by five men dressed in thawbs, two seemingly in their twenties, the others middle-aged. Loaded semiautomatic machine guns, strewn casually about, surround our circle as we engage in lively conversation, speaking a language unknown to me. The dream state slows, and suddenly

I am no longer separate from the language but inside it, and it is alive. Part of me is startled by the language gusting through me—sounds borne by the same air that nourishes the arid landscape rolling from the back of my throat, produced by muscles used in uncustomary ways.

I feel many forces of evolution at work, so unexpected, numerous, and revitalizing that they give rise to symphonies in my nervous system, enlivening the most silent parts of my being. Sounds reverberate within as when a bow is drawn across the open strings of a violin, and words grow roots through which archetypal forces within them are projected into the space in which we are all huddled together.

Upon awakening just before dawn, with my throat hoarse and my neck muscles taut, I have the strangest sense of humanity's origins. I am a citizen of a very remote country that was once here. Thought is motionless, simple. Bone-weary as I am, I tingle from crown to foot. A presence fills me then works through my body. Tears fall as I am moved by this new openness and sense of connectedness to archetypal forces through language. I decide my tears are what I carry of ocean and that perhaps we must become ocean, giving ourselves to it, if we are to be transformed.

Over the next weeks, four more illuminations of this nature occur, all situated in war-torn countries—Iraq, Egypt, Syria, Somalia—where individuals are conversing in back alleys, bombed-out houses, underground huts, and tunnels. During each illumination, I experience merging with the native language, its vibrating sound permeating my inner being while the external world recedes. Just before I feel myself becoming language, time slows down and my consciousness changes. Simultaneously, a subtle emotion fills me from the roots of my hair to my heels. My awareness is absorbed first into the internal sound then into vastness, like stars as they shine. Repeatedly, archetypal forces behind words invade the spaces and I'm imbued with a palpable sense of knowing. The surroundings, like vessels, suddenly fill with lucidity. I feel both a heightening of sensation and a structural and qualitative change in awareness.

I wonder, what is this seizure of the flesh by the vibrations of sound? It is as if the delicate

nerve fibers of the plexus, or ganglia, are sub-
jected to a hammering, as if I am a song being
sung or a stringed instrument being played. The
spirit, no longer a trespasser in the territory of
matter, is now a creator in the field of matter. All
five illuminations, I realize, portray some latent
force being born into the visible world through
language.

One day there is an unexpected knock at the front
door. It is my friend Richard, retired from NASA
and now living in Duluth, two and half hours
north of Minneapolis. He routinely appears out
of nowhere, bringing staples for my sustenance as
if I were incapable of supplying my own. I am
excited to see him; I know he will welcome a conversational walk together, and I want to tell him
about my latest illuminations and my recent experiences in Peru. His presence soothes my feelings
of alienation whenever I return from the Andes con-
fused by our culture, which seems oblivious to its
surroundings—the minute gestures of plants and
animals, the speech of birds, the taste of winds, the

smells of soil—as if cut off from nature by reflective glass. By contrast, Richard and I heed the sensory surround-sound of the moment.

As we stroll outdoors in silence, the moist ground under our feet gives a little, making me feel connected to nature. Finally bringing myself to speak, I blurt out, "The living light I have experienced recently could only have come from God."

Richard smiles and remarks, "You have had more illuminations?"

Sliding my arm into his to steady myself as we walk, I share the latest ones and add, "Richard, in all five occurrences some transcendent force was moving through the space and everyone present partook in it. Time seemed to stop; silence fell on everything. Thinking ceased; feeling was enhanced; and meaning was palpable, filling the self and leaving no room for anything else."

"I wonder why they all took place in war-torn Middle Eastern countries," he says.

Shrugging, I reply, "I don't know. I'm a woman of peace, not revolution."

He is thoughtful then announces, "The wind within a person is in no way autonomous. It's in continual interchange with the surrounding winds and is part of the eternal wind itself."

"Yes, I know," I say, smiling. "There would be you, who spent twenty years at NASA; my former partner in Landstuhl, Germany, managing the US ICU hospital receiving troops from the Benghazi attack; and my younger brother, a lieutenant colonel in the US Army, currently stationed at the White House on Obama's national security team. Likely, I am not separate from these winds."

Richard replies, "Maybe it is because you are a language lover, as well as a freedom sycophant, and a new light frequency is emerging on the planet. Or maybe you *are* a woman of revolution—a language revolution." We both laugh heartily, though I can't deny the possible truth of his remark. We continue our walk in silence, enveloped in the symphonic sounds of nature.

Soon after we return home, Richard departs for Duluth. I slice one of the Pink Lady apples he brought, place it on a plate with a huge dollop of organic cashew butter, and take it out to the yard, eager to resume my immersion in nature's musical composition. As I bite into the apple slices bursting with juice, I think to myself: Through a lifetime of lucid dreaming, I have become accustomed to registering the manifestation of dreams in the everyday world. What is new for me now are the strange changes in my body and my awareness, resulting from the language illuminations. An insistence in my body, in no way self-created, becomes palpable when I'm quietly reading or listening to a conversation, and linger over a word or phrase.

I'm especially surprised by the effects showing up more and more during conversational exchanges with others, including in my work as a spiritual teacher consulting with clients. Never before have I been filled with such delicate and encompassing vibrations, or felt my body could receive such a degree of influence. No longer can I even distinguish which sense is receiving these strong and persistent communications. I am clearly being guided into a deepening relationship with language, qualitatively and dimensionally. Language seems more alive the more sensitive the silken web of my sensory system becomes. And the more atoms of my body that are touched, the more different planes of awareness appear to unfold. My adventures with language transcending everyday realities are revealing a subterranean reservoir of wisdom from which the internal logician is exiled yet awareness expands. I now find language to be a "probe" sent to the outer reaches of human experience, prompting expansions in awareness. It seems to liberate within me an alluring pull into life and consequently is intensely enlivening, while giving glimpses of the interconnectedness of all things.

Wandering back into the house, I put away the staples Richard brought and reflect on my circumstances. Having been hustled by death, I am no longer victimized by life. Yet, still permeated by emptiness, I know not how to proceed. Prior to this time, I traveled the world and, for twenty-five years, had been intimately connected to the Q'ero culture of the high Andes. I delivered book talks and keynote addresses; facilitated spiritual retreats; and maintained a consulting practice. Now I don't see any of these activities as important. Meanwhile, everyday small tasks seem to reveal a trace of eternity.

Richard calls to let me know he is home then announces, "You are given these illuminations for a purpose, yet you hide them."

I want to reply, "Is that a question or a pronouncement?" Instead, I soften and say, "I never seek them, yet they come. I have become possessed by something and know not what it is. The illuminations seize me and will not let go, tilling hard ground into soft soil."

He responds, "I like that image. Good night, beloved Christina." I hang up and, remembering the moist ground yielding underfoot during our walk, feel myself yielding a little too. I realize that undergoing encounters with living language not of my own making involves not only receiving them but submitting to them. This occurs while allowing myself to experience language without conceptualizing and thereby cutting off the potent and mysterious energy it projects.

It is now dark. There is a strong wind, accompanied intermittently by the lash of rain, which shakes and excites my nervous system. The storm thunders on the house then stops, leaving deep silences between torrents of rainfall. In the dark I undress and slide into bed, covering my face with blankets, feeling the safety and warmth of my breath. As I fall asleep, I surrender to the darkness within me, remembering that it, too, is fecund soil containing seeds of new possibility.

4

Interior Trapdoors

When interior trapdoors open,
permitting us to experience hidden possibilities
of language, we become aware of other times,
places, and states of being.

SITTING AT MY DESK AT DAWN, I feel the dull throb of a headache. I'm unable to write the last of a ten-part audio series titled The Global Heart, which should land in the listener like a breeze blowing through trees thick with leaves, tendering movement. Gazing out the window, I am distracted by a soundless voice telling me I'm impeded because my real work with the illuminations is just beginning, that thus far I have done little more than experience them while, as language's mouthpiece, I must also reveal them to others. I suspect that doing so would at once demonstrate and manifest language's potential for expanding awareness.

When inspiration for writing eludes me, I seek a change of scene. No need to travel far; a trip to the literary realm will suffice. So when the local library opens I go there. I tell the librarian: "Jacquie, I am fond of the twentieth-century German poet Rainer Maria Rilke and am looking for a book describing his views on language. Rilke's works invariably bring me to a sensory experience with unseen forces, and now I'm curious about his relationship to language itself."

"I'll see what I can find," she responds. Shortly after, she asks, "Have you read *Proust and Rilke: The Literature of Expanded Consciousness* by E. F. N. Jephcott? It follows both authors' development in writing and how their consciousness changed as they explored language. I can order it through interlibrary loan. It may be a couple weeks or so."

Enthralled by the possibility of reading such a treasure, I thank her for the recommendation, adding, "I'm going to purchase a copy for myself." I walk home and order a used copy from a bookstore that specializes in rare titles.

The book arrives five days later, beautifully wrapped and smelling musty like a vintage volume. I sit down, put my glasses on, and peruse the introduction and first chapter. A wave of primal hesitancy undulates through me as I am surprised by the author's use of a term identical to the one I've been using to describe my own experiences with language: "privileged moments." He writes, "The moment is particularly difficult to define; it will therefore be necessary to quote extensively from descriptions of privileged moments by a number of writers."[1] I stand up, propelled by an eerie feeling of foreshadowing that makes me want to close the book. Something moves house inside me. I have the absurd sense, both mentally and physically, that one interior living space has been replaced by another. It is as if an unfamiliar guest has entered, rearranged things, and all I have grown accustomed to has disappeared.

Three days pass before I return to the book. Just before dawn on day four I stumble upon the following passage from Rilke's novel *The Notebooks of Malte Laurids Brigge*, describing the main character's experience with language, which many scholars feel reflects the author's:

Visual and sensory awareness of reality is
undergoing a transformation....everything
goes deeper into me and does not stop
where it used to. Normal limits of awareness
disappear, and one experiences an
unrestricted openness to impressions....In
this state one no longer experiences time as
chronological succession, but as "total time."[2]

And then:

I fear this change with a nameless fear....I am
in the grip of a force beyond my control....
Despite my fear I am like someone who has a
great event before him, and I remember that
I used often to have a similar feeling before
I began to write. But now the experience is
so extreme....I shall be written....I am the
impression which will change. I should console
myself with the knowledge that it is not
impossible to see everything differently, and
yet to live.[3]

Closing the book, I gaze out the window of my
study, stunned at the similarities between Rilke's

descriptions and my experiences with the illuminations. I note how Rilke, too, must have felt in the
grip of a force beyond his control, one in which
sensory experience of the spoken and written word
went deeper into him than ever before, revealing
new dimensions of reality.

I wander onto the deck in my backyard and
stand quietly watching tree branches sway, hearing
songbirds begin to forage, their chirps still soft as
the stars yield to the dawn. In this quiet interlude
where thought has subsided, a fiery light unexpectedly permeates my brain and inflames my heart,
simultaneously blinding and illuminating me. As
the light passes through me increasingly without
resistance, my body feels almost porous. Around
me is a stillness in which everything is moving.
There is no me or trees, birds or clouds, only an
awareness of the movement of all things at once
singing throughout the molecules of my nearly
immobile body. Then comes wave upon wave of
uncontainable energy.

As the illumination fades, I feel radiant, preg-
nant with a million stars. I begin to hiccup uncontrollably, amazed to think a fragment of eternity

may have become lodged in my body. An immense feeling of serenity then trickles over me. I wonder if I am perhaps undergoing a modification in human adaptation. Just as some species instantly grew gills and others wings, I conclude, my experiences with language, during which conceptual thought ceases and awareness increases, could perhaps portend a future avenue to elevated consciousness. I wander back into the house and, after flopping down in my living room chair, suddenly remember that I have a consultation with a new client in two hours and need to prepare.

Upon arriving at my office, I see my client in the waiting room. He is a twenty-nine-year-old referred by his primary care physician because he has been having difficulty concentrating at work and feels depressed. Inviting him into my consulting room, I note that his spirit hangs on him like limp clothes on a scarecrow. I offer him tea, observing his seem-ingly taciturn demeanor as he responds with very short answers to my social courtesies.

As I sit across from him, cognizant of a Kleenex box perfectly positioned on the table beside him, he mumbles, "I wanted to cancel today's appointment but decided this isn't the worst place to be. Besides, you might be able to explain why I feel numb."

Nodding, I reply, "People often mistake numbness for nothingness, but numbness isn't an absence of feelings; it's a response to being overwhelmed by too many feelings."

He looks at the floor, yet I can see I've got his full attention. He glances toward his cell phone, which is vibrating, but I resist the urge to follow his gaze. I stay with him so he doesn't get pulled away, retreating into numbness whenever his unwanted feelings appear.

Returning his attention to me, he aloofly utters, "I don't know what to say."

To help him settle into the consultation, I reply, "You said this isn't the worst place to be. What's the worst?"

He shrugs his shoulders in a dull torpor. I welcome his resistance, viewing it as a clue to where the crux of the work lies. He then announces, impassively, "The worst place would be in the same room as my mother."

As he speaks, the habit of my mind to sweep along drawing conclusions is thwarted and my attention is instead carried inward. There I am amazed to notice a shadow pattern of the forces emanating from his spoken words, their roots secured in matrices that are also inside me; it is as though an interior trapdoor has opened to grant me this new somatic awareness. I can feel the fibers and tissues of these root systems inside me, absorbing sensation for their sustenance. And I can feel space losing its structural coherence, becoming a synthesis of times, places, and states of being as occurred during my exchange with the boy at the tribute for Mother Teresa in Montana.

Then my client spontaneously volunteers, "I am having problems in my relationship with my girlfriend." Tearing up, he adds, "I think I have a masturbation addiction, and now I can't come when I'm having sex with her." Then, wiping his nose and eyes on his sleeve, he becomes more untethered. With his head now down near his knees, he confides, "Sometimes I can't seem to separate my girlfriend from my mother." Hues of crimson appear in his face as unadulterated rage rises in him. I decide to remain quiet. Time seems to stop, and a silence falls on everything in the room. My thinking stops too, yet my awareness intensifies, making the primal energy behind his experience so palpable I can sense it flooding the room and my inner landscape, leaving space for nothing else. We are both immersed in some deep baptismal waters.

Suddenly, all six feet, two inches of him pitch forward off the couch to his hands and knees, and he sobs uncontrollably. I know to let the moment run its course. When he finally gathers himself back onto the couch, our session has neared its end. I can tell that whatever happened in our shared moment exceeded his expectations as well as mine. Knowing he is going back out into the world, I softly introduce a little levity, whispering, "Well, I think maybe you have begun healing your numbness." He chuckles.

I assure him that everything he shared often goes along with a masturbation addiction in young men and that he could heal from this in time. Before leaving, he mumbles, "I feel naked and seen."

I close the door and ponder whether the peculiar state I experienced influenced the exchange. Had some ensouled force moving through the room impacted us both, I wonder. As with the Middle East illuminations, mental activity was almost nonexistent, yet awareness deepened while spoken words surged into an inner boundlessness. Was the language of our surface exchange beseeching us to become more conscious of it to free it from its societal moorings, I ask myself. What is clear is that I entered a different reality, feeling it throughout my being.

Before the next client is to arrive, I check my phone and discover a request to reschedule our session because of an emergency vet appointment. I am relieved, since the expanded boundaries of my awareness have left me searching for the comfort of homeostasis.

Hesitant to drive home in this state, I make a cup of chamomile tea, keenly aware of feeling unmoored. Before this morning, the confines of my awareness had been like a house I knew to the last nook, its forms, advantages, drawbacks appearing to be those of my own body. But now, having accidently sprung open some interior trapdoor, I am wandering through countless mysterious rooms that seem like home to my soul. Simultaneously, I seem to be leaving behind a being who observes, judges, and evaluates.

Sipping the tea, I reflect on how sensory cues have us immediately conceptualizing rather than experiencing. Words, however, have infinite depth and, like colors, awaken somatic-sensory receptors, all the while honoring margins of the inarticulate. Thus, what at first seems simply to be a stream of emitted words becomes a quality of consciousness. As such, its message can be received, for it is now in an inner space of sensory experience—no longer in the space between the ears, home to concepts, ideas, and theories. I remind myself that when interior trapdoors open and our awareness expands to other times, places, and states of being, we see firsthand what language can offer humanity.

I now feel ready to drive home in rush hour traffic. My conceptualizing mind, well conditioned, is happy not to be extinct. My body appreciates the calm of homeostasis yet notes the loss of a deeper connection with the world and its sublime joy. As I sit in traffic, I imagine living language delivering troves of strange life forces. I picture it flowing from a voice or pen into us when interior trapdoors open, then continuing into the past or future on its return to silence. Living language, I conclude, is more than a means by which humans communicate; it is a transmission of spirit through the coexistence of the temporal with the eternal. Never is its expression inert, like much of human communication; instead, like wind blowing in trees thick with leaves, it moves eternally.

5

Rilke's "Total Time"

*When somatic-sensory experience of the spoken
or written word goes deeper into us, not stopping
where it used to, new dimensions of reality are
revealed.... Language is embodied, as thought
gives way to direct perception.*

AT 1:30 A.M., I AWAKE, rise, sling a light wool sweater
around my shoulders, and head downstairs to my
home office. I open the window a crack. The jeweled constellation Orion is ascending and will reach
its zenith in an hour. I place Beethoven's *Fidelio* on
the CD player, knowing that one of the glories of
this opera is the sonority of the orchestra's basses
and low strings.

While absorbed in strains of Beethoven, I hear
my cell phone ring. It is Rosa in Cusco, Peru, letting

me know that Miguel, my eight-year-old Q'ero godson, is lost in the Andes at an elevation of 20,000 feet, having become separated from a group three days earlier while shepherding alpaca. I know the situation is dire by the way my heart drops like a stone and my knees tremble beneath me. I tell myself to remain calm.

I call my beloved friend of thirty years and part-time assistant, Sheri, to help me navigate the situation. "Is everything okay?" she asks, sounding worried. When I am silent for too long, she adds, "Chris, do I need to come to your house?"

I find my words, saying, "No, I'll be okay," then explain the situation. Hesitantly, I tell her, "I feel the need to get on a plane and be there."

I hear her swallow hard, apprehensive about me traveling to Peru after my bout with yellow fever. Following a long pause, she concedes, "I think you need to go too." Despite the hour, she shifts with light-ning speed into organizational mode, announcing, "I will find you a flight out tomorrow; call your house sitter in the morning to check on her availability; and, if there's time, pick up a few gifts for the Q'ero chil-dren." Sheri is a consummate soul of service to youth.

We end our conversation with her saying, "I trust you will pack accordingly." It was more a question than a statement. She knows by now that packing for this high-altitude destination with no amenities requires care.

I reply, "Yes, indeed. Thank you, and I love you."

By early morning, Sheri has secured a flight; hired Abby, my favorite house sitter, to care for Patchabella and Princess Yowls-A-Lot, my Siberian husky and Hawaiian calico cat; and picked up thirty pairs of little fleece gloves from two different gas stations for the Q'ero children. She drops by the house to deliver the gifts before heading to her job as a social worker at a Minneapolis Public High School.

By late afternoon, I'm on a plane to Lima, then Cusco. When I arrive eighteen hours later, Rosa and her husband, Ricardo, pick me up at the airport and drive me to their home.

"*Ven* (Come in)," Rosa says, motioning me into the small dirt-floored living room. Ricardo is a local healer, and their living room is his clinic. In the room are a table covered with herbs and oils, and numerous chairs occupied by locals waiting to be seen. On a small cot in the center is an Indian woman having postbirth complications. Candles are everywhere—stumps of beeswax with wicks, red Christmas tapers, tea lights in small glass tumblers. But not one is lit. Only an incandescent lightbulb hanging on a wire from the ceiling diffuses the shadows cast by the late afternoon sunlight streaming through the room's one window.

Rosa brings me a cup of hot coca tea and a soft alpaca wool poncho for warmth. I sit on a sack of cornhusks in the corner of the room, wrapping myself in the poncho, my head resting against the whitewashed adobe wall, feeling the solemnity of the moment. In repose, I listen to my silent thoughts: "Miguel, may you be safe. We will find you soon." I realize the thoughts are a prayer and prayer for me has always been about releasing my defenses against the natural motion of life. Images of my time with Miguel saturate me: the Q'ero godmother ritual in which I gave Miguel, at age two, his first ceremonial haircut; holding him on my lap while teaching him to read; learning each other's native language; and him sleeping next to Santi and me, with his small arms resting over us and his dog Tayta by his other side.

After a few minutes of prayer and reflection, I experience light with such intensity that movement becomes impossible. Then I perceive a sound softer than physical tones. As I float with it, I hear:

Calm yourself and hear each of these words.

The
  mind
   is
    still.
     The
      heart
       is
        open.
Seek
 the
  light
   behind
    all
     that
      is.

Each word is dropped into a vat of palpable silence. The sequence is repeated. Time slows, and I feel each word spreading out in space, becoming interwoven with it. Meanings recede, and each word becomes a world resonating with the boundless silence. My body, motionless, is vibrantly alive.

As the silence deepens, I feel my customary analytical consciousness dissolving, along with my usual insistence on explanations. I am now inside a reverberating field, in the presence of a generative act that both includes and encompasses me—a place where word becomes spirit. So expansive is this state that it feels as if the cosmos is inside me.

Now the words begin to attach themselves to other elements in the room—objects, people, the wind that pierces the adobe walls, the breath of the woman on the cot, the corners of the space shrouded in darkness. It is as though they are feeling through me and I through them. Each element is no longer distinct but in a continuous flow, including the interplay between me and the other elements, all forming a whole. I sense an exquisite musical harmony in the exchanges between my inner and outer worlds. As the illumination fades,

I'm reminded of T. S. Eliot's homage to music "heard so deeply that it isn't heard at all, but you are the music while the music lasts."[1]

As dawn approaches, I feel gusts of wind enter the house and take some of the life of the woman on the cot, who is now barely alive, her eyes set, her breath shallow and rattling. I hear Rosa in the kitchen packing wholesome food and remedies for today's ascent to Miguel's village of Chua Chua at 18,000 feet. Our plan is for me—having spent a day acclimating to the altitude of Cusco—to drive with Ricardo to the territory of Nacion Q'ero, then as far as the road will take us, where my Q'ero friend Simone will be waiting to accompany me up the mountain to join in the search for Miguel. It was Simone and his wife who had taken Miguel in, along with his mangy dog, Tayta, after yellow fever had thwarted my mission to ensure my godson would remain in the care of the medicine lineage following his parents' death.

Soon Ricardo and I drive the six hours to meet Simone at the end of the road, which is more like an alpaca trail. Then Simone and I begin our trek, with plans to camp overnight before going to Miguel's village. As we walk in silence, rain begins to fall lightly then pours in torrents. Lightning strikes fill the sky. We find shelter under a granite outcrop protective enough to keep us semi-dry while devouring avocados, potatoes, and boiled eggs. We sleep sitting upright with our backs against the rock. As sleep descends upon me, I am encompassed by another light, and sounds of occasional avalanches from nearby mountains jar the ground. Unexpectedly, I see a vision of Miguel in his poncho curled up in a fetal position, with Tayta lying beside him, near an old Incan altar ruin, snow beginning to blanket him, his breath shallow, like the woman's on the cot. Beneath my terror at seeing him in this state is a pervasive sense that our existences are deeper and vaster than our suffering. The air around him fills like a vessel with a light that seems to indicate higher life. I drink in its richness and immediately sense my awareness expanding to embrace a harmony that transcends time and space. Past and future are now an integral part of the present, every moment enfolding the earth and the heavens. I feel linked to wind, snow, Miguel, Incan ruins, and death. I am in them, and they are inside me.

At first light of day, the storm subsides, and a barely audible rhythmic drizzle sates the dawn in sorrow. Knowing the outcome of last night's snowstorm that awaits us a few thousand feet farther up the mountain, I murmur to Simone in Quechua, "Miguel died of cold last night." I do not know the word for exposure. Simone speaks in Spanish so that I understand his reply, saying, "*Si, escuchas los muros de un ser humano, aunque seas tú mismo, escucharás el canto de la tierra.* (Yes, if you listen at the walls of one human being, even if that one is yourself, you will hear the song of earth.)" The Q'ero see the earth everywhere, I remind myself, both inside and outside themselves: in the faces of their children, in the wind that carries the rain-bearing clouds, in the sacred rivers that flow through the land, nourishing vegetation. Miguel once said to me, "I hear the potatoes grow in the earth. Every day they change." Santi similarly remarked, "The earth lives more quietly inside you." I've searched all my life for this older world that was lost to me, this world my body now remembers.

Simone and I make our way to the village of Chua Chua, one of five Q'ero villages between

18,000 and 22,000 feet. The huts are hard to see from our path as we climb amidst the clouds, making it seem we are moving toward a wild, uncertain destination, though it is one I have been coming to for many years. Miguel's childhood hut— which he, Santi, and I shared—has been prepared for me. Twenty or thirty candles have transformed the windowless thatched-roof rock home into a chapel. Although it is bone-chilling cold, the room radiates warmth from the many candles insulating it from the spring snowstorm. Simone goes to meet the Q'ero elders gathered near an old half-buried, crumbling Incan structure reclaimed by meadow grass, while I remain in the hut. Peeling off my wet clothes, I wrap myself in three heavy alpaca wool blankets and before long succumb to a pounding headache aggravated by rolling nausea and the gravity of the circumstances.

A day later Miguel's lifeless body is found precisely as depicted in my vision. Hearing the news, I know the appropriate protocol is to join the Q'ero people beloved to me, yet I remain for some time in the hut, immobilized by heartache and misery. Bereft following the passing of Miguel, Santi, and

other beloved villagers so recently, I feel warmed in
the candlelit hut among the Q'ero people and safe
in the arms of solitude. Yearning now to speak to
the silence, I whisper:

> In every human being I love, there is
> something of you. And I seek you. The best
> and the noblest part of the man whose light
> you kindled in me is now with you, as is my
> godson. Left behind is a worn-out husk in
> the small room in which I experienced the
> greatest and deepest happiness of my life.
> Standing here, I find you have placed me
> before your ultimate mystery. May I have
> the strength to know and accept that there
> is no answer. I need patience. Life will be
> difficult for a while.

It is my desire to leave Miguel's poncho where I
left Santi's following his death, at a sacred Incan
altar in Q'Ollpacucho, the ceremonial village of
the Q'ero living at 21,000 feet. I was presented with
Santi's poncho and worn-out sandals made from

ENCOUNTERS WITH LIVING LANGUAGE

recycled tires (a Q'ero favorite), both of which he had been wearing at the time of his death by lightning. When they were given to me, I could still smell the remnants of fire and see a hole burned through the rubber of the left heel by the strike. Cherishing what remained of Santi, I hiked up to Q'Ollpacucho with Simone and lovingly placed Santi's sandals, wrapped inside his poncho, at the old Incan ceremonial altar overlooking the valley where he and I would go when he worried about the fate of the Q'ero nation.

Now I want to leave Miguel's poncho there, but I can't make the climb due to altitude sickness. I communicate my wishes to Simone, who takes Miguel's poncho and agrees to make the ascent. Since Simone was also the caretaker of Miguel and he, too, lost his good friend Santi, I know this undertaking will help bring him closure. Feeling complete, I descend the mountain with several young Q'ero men.

Upon arrival in Cusco, I once again board a flight to the United States. Looking out the window, I envision death as a silent sharer in all life's processes. I know that Santi, Miguel, and I remain united and that the constellation of forces holding us closely together, having visibly terminated, persists more powerfully deep down in the invisible realm, where it endures as a vein of gold more constant than a star. As the fabric of these times slips over me with its interweavings of temporal events, I see, outside the window, streaming tendrils of air that make me suddenly aware of how invisible currents carry us this way and that; I smile, thinking these currents, like death's invisible yet formative presence in life, are too often ignored and we mistakenly assume we are controlling our own lives by making sporadic decisions until one day, like pieces of a quilt, everything suddenly comes together.

Pondering the notion of death in life, I flash on a dream I had twenty-two years ago. In the dream I was at Heathrow Airport in London, where three men and a woman asked if I would deliver a package to the United States. The package was a wooden box, five feet long, eighteen inches wide, a foot high. One of the men unlatched three wood fasteners and slowly opened the box. Inside, on top of an old, delicate tan textile, lay a mummy adorned in gold jewelry, one foot tucked under the other, body and head perfectly straight, eye sockets hypnotizing. I awoke from the dream as if I had eaten a piece of it. Shortly thereafter I traveled to the high Andes of Peru and for the first time met the Q'ero Indians, descendants of the Inca. Another year passed before I realized the mummy adorned with gold in the dream was Incan. Fourteen more years passed before I discovered that the woman in the dream at Heathrow Airport was to become the editor of my first book, *Transcendent Dreaming: Stepping into Our Human Potential*; she is now archiving the language illuminations. More than a couple decades have passed since that dream. I've witnessed a dying culture in accordance with Q'ero prophecy. The contents of that wooden box—a foreshadowing of the future—came back with me to the United States.

Considering a trip to the bathroom, I glance at the middle-aged woman sitting next to me on the plane and see the title of the book she is reading: *In the Company of Rilke*, by Stephanie Dowrick. It is a book I very much enjoyed. We have a short chat about it before she returns to reading. I feel in my bones what Rilke called "total time"—no longer experiencing time as a succession of chronological moments—and why he was so deeply affected while experiencing expanding consciousness occasioned by language. Indeed, when somatic-sensory experience of the spoken or written word goes deeper into us, not stopping where it used to, new dimensions of reality are revealed.

I'm convinced, after the illumination in Cusco, that using the lens of language to give order to experience is not the only way to perceive the experience. In the absence of conceptual thought, the body, still active, registers intense sensations, another means of perception. As thought gives way to this sort of experiential perception, language becomes embodied, producing a level of awareness far beyond normal. Such a shift affects the way reality is perceived and also how aspects of it are connected: elements entering into this new relationship with our sensibilities become "musicalized," resonating with one another. Then as consciousness further expands to embrace the external world, the physical and mental spheres are perceived as inseparable, and soon the notion of a self separate from others disappears, giving way to a sense of harmony between inner and outer worlds and of embracing the whole of existence. Ultimately awareness expands even more, as mine has during this time in Miguel's remote village, connecting the present to moments in the past or future through instances of sensation.

Once again anchored in the present, I can feel eternity—the never-ending present moment—becoming a physical experience. As we begin our descent for landing, I realize that, strange as it may be, this understanding makes the death of loved ones more bearable.

6

Language's Mistress

Who knew language could render
such an incandescent affection for life
as a whole, an affection no longer reserved
for incarnate lovers?

I WELCOME THE DOUBLE-CLICK sound the key makes when it unlocks my front door. Expecting to feel relief, I'm surprised by the uneasiness inside me as I enter my home. Everything looks temporary. On the fireplace mantel, Abby has left a freshly picked bouquet of white phlox from the perennial garden that already shows signs of wilt.

To soothe my discomfort, I spend hours in my urban yard. Late autumn debris lies heavy on the earth. I sense the winter winds about to roll in, while inside me winter already exists. I cut back the grapevines, the unripe fruit on dying vines reminding me of Miguel's death at such a young age. Something about clipping back the vines consoles me, as though in doing so I am preparing them and myself for new life. The familiar presence of Patchi and Princess taking in the autumn air brings comfort too. Resting for a moment, I look toward the sky and watch two ravens noisily warbling in the silver maple tree. I smell the faint scent of the tree rearing up against the weight of the sky and know that at the heart of aloneness I am intimately connected to life.

Suddenly, I am enclosed within a luminous sphere. The sky then opens to a broad expanse of blue vibrating like a sonorous crystal or an awakening. Gazing at its immenseness seems to enlarge the muscles of my body. Latin words slowly emerge audibly from somewhere inside me one at a time—verbs, nouns, adjectives, articles, prepositions—pulsating while projected onto the sky:

> *quaguaversal*
> *solivagant*
> *vagary*
> *personare*
> ....

Each word, like a surge of incipient life, oscillates, slowly builds to a crescendo, then recedes.

There is a low continuous noise, that of silence itself, which encompasses everything and awakens every cell of my body—a palpable vacuum. The sound of each word imprints itself on the silence. I sense my body is not an entity that exists separate from the world; rather, it is interwoven with the inner and outer currents of silence.

I experience the aliveness of the words, following them to the farthest reaches of fathomless space, home to the contexts that gave rise to them. The syllables and rhythms seem to penetrate far below conscious levels of thought, and they take something back on their return to their origins. I feel a connection with what has been forgotten, perhaps for centuries—my surroundings. The sky, the crisp air, the noisy ravens, and me all form a whole.

A further portal opens through reverberations that move like currents, and the universe begins to flow through me. I am entangled in the substance of the words, which chime like bells from all directions, as the spaces inside and outside my body become one and the air and my body awaken in unison.

The words create a sense of depth, while the irregular intervals between them give an impression of transparency, both enhancing my perspective. Suddenly, I am an effect of the light, the only force that moves. The universe is laid out like a meal presented on a textured tablecloth. Extremes recognize and greet each other in an act of creation. A strange, marvelous hunger inside me rejoices, bathed in ineffable presences. In this moment, God is not implausible. I feel in my marrow a silent invocation: "To what can be, to what shall be." Then the huge sky sneezes into me, reconstituting my body, which can scarcely bear the panicky sensation of its nakedness. My body stretches, seeking the torsion and tension needed to reestablish its state of readiness. Simultaneously, my mind slowly reestablishes its former condition, replete with worries, anxieties, contemplation.

I enter the house, close the door behind me, and lean against it. As the godlike qualities dissipate, I feel a return to my everyday self, melancholic yet grateful for the realization that a new modification is apparently occurring in the quality of my awareness. I have an inkling words may be virtual cups of light, giving us capabilities to experience other times, places, and states of being, then ultimately becoming chalices of inner awareness.

I wonder, have we been unable to experience this—the true essence of language—because we expected words to do no more than refer to and describe things? Although persistent habits of perception dominate contemporary culture, particularly the Newtonian-Cartesian tendency to see life-forms as separate from one another, clearly there are other means of perception that allow us to penetrate dimensions inconceivable, unconditional, and eternal, I tell myself. I am reminded of Sufi master Hazrat Inayat Khan, who says:

> If a pebble is thrown into the sea, it puts the water in action. One hardly stops to think to what extent this vibration acts upon the sea. What one can see in the little waves and circles that the pebble produces before one, one sees only these. But the vibration that it has produced in the sea reaches much further than one can imagine. What we call "space" is a much finer world. If we call it "sea," it is a sea with the finest fluid. If we call it "land," it

is a land that is incomparably more fertile
than the land we know. It takes in everything,
and it allows to grow that which one's eyes
do not see, one's ears do not hear.[1]

I find this new land in the body incomparably more
fertile than the land I've known. And I imagine the
two spanning a realm that could be a place for living
an enhanced life.

Ceremoniously, I make matcha tea. While still
trying to master the panicky sensation of being, I
develop an insidious headache. Exasperated, I take
a shower, then bestow an abject meal of damp left-
over lung before Princess, take the garbage out,
and, by 7:00 p.m., retreat to my bedroom.

Lifting the book I'm currently reading from
my nightstand, *The World Is Sound* by Joachim
Ernst-Berendt, I peruse five pages and am surprised to see mention of one of the pulsating Latin
words that showed up in the illumination earlier in
the day. I read:

The Great Tone is the tone of being…the
tone from which God made the world, which

continues to sound at the bottom of creation, and which sounds through everything. In Latin, the term meaning to sound through something is *personare*. If nothing sounds through from the bottom of being, a human being is human biologically, at best, but is not a per-son, because he does not live through the son (the tone, the sound). He does not live the sound which is the world.[2]

After this serendipitous encounter, I am left with the inexplicable noise of silence, a sensation as impenetrable as color.

Upon awakening at dawn, I shuffle into the kitchen to make strong French Roast coffee. Pouring a cup, I sit down at the dining room table. Princess sits on a chair, looking indignant with mute feline reproach. The experience of yesterday afternoon comes back with a curious aftertaste. Nothing tangible has changed, yet everything has changed. Mentally, I seem far away, my sense of space and time modified.

I am called to return to passages by Rilke from E. F. N. Jephcott's book and stumble upon lines I underscored that reflect Rilke's similar experience with language:

> I experience myself no longer through self-consciousness in the normal way, but through my impressions of the outside world. External reality becomes a kind of metaphor for my own existence.[3]

Likewise, yesterday, through an experience with language, I felt external reality to be as much a part of myself as my own thoughts, my inner life giving way to a feeling of universal participation.

Another underscored passage seems to describe my own unsettling feeling of separation from everyday reality while being pulled into a more expansive existence:

> I pass through a crisis—something is going on in me that is beginning to separate and cut me off from everything. I am leaving behind my formal personality and the familiar world to

which it belonged. I am now filled with
fear by the sense of losing contact with my
familiar world. I fear this change with a
nameless fear. I have not yet got used to this
world, which seems good to me. What am
I to do in another one?[4]

It brings me solace to know that Rilke also was apprehensive about sensing separation from everyday reality. Although it is unnerving to be aware of myself leaving behind a familiar way of relating to the world, the attendant feeling of universal participation and interconnectedness is inviting.

Curiously, I realize that while inconsolable with grief over the loss of loved ones, I've somehow become language's mistress. Like other mistresses, I'm living a secret life in the margins of society. When an illumination occurs, like a lover it cleaves as though skin to skin, affecting every sense simultaneously. It envelops me in an awareness that is unsettling, yet suddenly releases me from the alienation experienced while passively observing, like a scream of liberation when making love. An immense harmony engulfs my soul. I feel in its plenitude an inexpressible comprehension of the wholeness of things, the abyss between me and objects closing until the differences vanish because we are all bathed in infinity. A subtle current passes from me into matter while life forces of the elements slowly pervade me, rising like sap, and I become nature, or nature becomes me in holy play, with unlimited joy. Who knew language could render such an incandescent affection for life as a whole, an affection no longer reserved for incarnate lovers. Is that why the illuminations are so capricious, flooding my consciousness unannounced then quickly ceasing, I wonder, leaving me arid?

A gentle rain begins falling outside the sliding glass patio door. I breathe the scent of unseen jasmine flowers and wonder about the sublime moments during which the mind loses the particularity that has kept it alert. I'm reminded of the young man in my office pitching forward off the couch, sobbing uncontrollably, and of the wintry squall portending Miguel's death. Gazing out the window, I feel tears of mourning fall down my face, washing away sorrow like the rain carrying away the late autumn debris and gifting me a new heart that beats in rhythm with the larger continuum. I see the loss of particularity as a sign of healing from blows dealt by fate.

7

Language's Openings to the Eternal

Extraordinary experiences with language
have somehow led me to a destiny
of incarnating the eternal in temporal time.

AT EARLY DAWN TWO DAYS after my last illumination, still feeling separation from everyday reality and an altered sense of space and time, I awaken from a dream in which I am in dialogue with an indigenous old woman I do not recognize. She whispers to me, "We are the same dream. We are as the water of the first days in pattern." Santi, sitting next to her, nods in agreement. I do not know the meaning of her words, yet the rhythm of her voice awakens within me a somatic-sensory awareness of the unseen pattern she speaks of. The dream ends with her stating, "The dream line must never ever be broken." I notice my feeling of "otherness" slowly evaporating, leaving in its wake an opening deep within me.

I try to fall back to sleep, but a wave of immense light pours into me, radiating an inexorable strength both within and around me. At its core lies complete tranquility, akin to the still center of a hurricane. Viewing it as an imperative, I get out of bed and walk the two steps to the window, where I see continuous lightning flashes unaccompanied by thunder. Still inwardly immobile, I have extreme lucidity, yet the more I try to access thought, the more stymied I am by fatigue. I rest in the chair next to my bed, where I find a small body beside me, warm and peacefully quiet. I nestle up to it gently; it nestles unknowingly up to me. I feel its hand move across its forehead, suddenly realizing the body is my own. There is a song of mutual gratitude to destiny for this moment of extreme harmony between my present self and my forth-coming self. Then there is a tearful return to ordinary consciousness. My heart melts.

I go back to bed, finding Patchi there upside down, all eighty-six pounds of her stretched seven feet long, legs extended in the air as if antennae.

While the moon shines through the skylight like a candle, a balm of sweet grief passes through my entire body. I relive what it was like to meet Santi's gaze. In his eyes, vast as space, I could see beyond time—always it was the same solemn hour, undivided into minutes, unmarked by timepieces. Santi, like all Q'ero Indians, did not live in linear time. For them, the past and future do not exist; they live in an eternal now. Nor does the self exist. They perceive the world through their senses without recognizing separate selves within it. As such, thoughts and ideas have little relevance. Because Santi and I did not speak each other's language well or share the experience of linear time and separate selves, our senses became lanterns illuminating our world. To know each other was to awaken in each other's depth and complexity.

Compelled by a desire to absorb the other, Santi and I shared a nocturnal custom. After the stars appeared, we would go outside the hut and lie on the earth, wrapped in an alpaca blanket. At 18,000 to 21,000 feet, there is a mysterious effect on one's being as clouds wander through such moments together and clusters of stars shimmer across space.

Everything nearby is invisible; everything seen in the distance, intangible. The stars made me feel irrelevant yet exquisitely alive. And in the darkness, which obscured the huts and the outlines of our bodies, there was no distinction between "I" and "non-I." Gazing at the stars while in Santi's arms, I would wonder whether individual lives were as transient as mayflies on a summer stream.

Simultaneously, there was the physical delight of body with body, a sensitive silent comprehension of one another. Santi would squeeze my left hand with his right, holding it long enough for my inner world to quiet. His breathing in and out in the silence made it seem like the cosmos was enclosed in his calm body. When we whispered to each other under our blanket, the ecstasy was more mountain sigh. There was a reach for something far beyond and way down underneath. The touching of our fingers when passing a cup of coca tea to each other, his adjustment of the neckline of my poncho, my brushing of earth from his hands made it obvious to me that I had surrendered my whole self to Santi and, in doing so, had begun to recognize openings to the eternal much like this morning's illumination involving my forthcoming self. Indeed, I could see myself as a magical point where time cedes its command to revelations of the perennial. In retrospect, I see my experiences with Santi—especially the stepping out of time and the disappearance of self in the universal no-self—as preparatory for receiving the illuminations that were soon to come. Always I will cherish my awakenings with him, a precious inheritance from our decade together on the planet.

An invisible, omnipresent, and formidable new beloved—language—is courting me now, I remind myself. And its advances are irresistible. The latest, articulated by the indigenous old woman in my dream, suggests, with Santi's concurrence, that I am being given illuminations for a purpose: to keep the "dream line" unbroken, a mission I do not fully understand. Even so, it does not escape me that her pronouncement about the "water of the first days" could refer to a new human consciousness, a magical point where the eternal is once again embodied in time.

Sitting up in bed, pillows propped behind me, I hear the wind blow leaves outside the window and see them swirl upward and away under the street-light. Autumn is making way for winter. I want to know where the wind gathers its strength so I can go there. The segment of my life in which the Andes was my home is over; some of my vigor is gone; and I would like to gather strength. Sitting here stripped of personal initiative, I experience a light so tangible I can feel it passing through my fingers, heralding a transformation within me—a sort of change in government. It appears that my actions will no longer be propelled by the same consciousness as before because my extraordinary experiences with living language have somehow led me to a destiny of incarnating the eternal in temporal time.

The consciousness springing from this encounter with living language is teaching me what it is like to embody the eternal—unseen forces that, coursing through the body, can unveil a deeper reality and arouse from its slumber a sense of the primordial life I share with all creation. Birdsong strikes my retina as a pageant of color. I smell the magical tones of the wind; I hear as a great fugue the repeated, harmonized greens of the forest, the cadence of stormy skies. There are indications of possible future circumstances long before they occur.

By late afternoon, I'm grateful for the slow, contemplative day. After getting the house in order and returning phone calls and emails, I read from *On Poetry and Poets* by T. S. Eliot, another writer who experienced privileged moments with language:

> All living things have their own laws of growth, which are not always reasonable, but must be accepted by the reason: things which cannot be neatly planned and put into order any more than the winds and the rains and the seasons can be disciplined.[1]

Reading Eliot's words, I realize that my experiences as a mistress of language have their own laws of growth and, though not always reasonable, must be accepted by reason just as the winds and the rains.

8

In the Bower of Language

Beneath every word, a mystery lies hidden.
Forces more inciting than inviting live here,
prompting each word, once inert like a fossil, to
unexpectedly light up new forms of awareness.

I'M LYING ON MY BACK in bed, supported by feather pillows, imbibing the moonlight before dawn. Outside the open window, there is a pause in the wind, and the stillness of the leaves affects me, transmitting revelations. Compelled to record what I see, hear, and feel in the moment, I go to my desk and write:

> I am in the bower of language, where language speaks, sings, and reveals other dimensions, perhaps beginning the farewell of its usage only to represent the world. I am experiencing the deeper nature of its essence—its dimensional,

or even quantum, capacity that moves us into expanded states of awareness. Beneath every word, a mystery lies hidden. Forces more inciting than inviting live here, prompting each word, once inert like a fossil, to unexpectedly light up new forms of awareness.

Then without warning I flash back to the Andes when, between life and death, I whispered to my great-grandmother, "The wind is never weary." Suddenly, I am buoyed up and spurred on by an impulse to again follow the current of clues about the deeper function of language. I feel impelled to return to the portion of E. F. N. Jephcott's book where he introduces characteristics of a privileged moment:

> A privileged moment has two essential characteristics: quality and the structure of awareness are changed. The qualitative change involves a heightening of sensations and of the apparent meaning they convey. The structural change involves a unification of all parts of awareness to form a total system. In embracing this unified system, the field

of consciousness expands far beyond its normal limits. Both these phenomena have been seen to be related to the absence of conceptual thought from consciousness.... But this conceptualizing faculty does not seem to be the only, or the first, of the mechanisms by which the mind gives order and unity to experience. In the absence of rational thought another, apparently autonomous, faculty is still active, and indeed its degree of activity seems to be in inverse proportion to that of the conceptualizing faculty.... This faculty, working autonomously, appears to be capable of producing in awareness a degree of unity and intensity far in excess of the needs of practical life.[1]

Reading these words leads me to think of meditation. When silence enters my meditation, its presence resonates throughout the fibers of the body, uniting me with the substance from which all things arise and return. Is this what Jephcott calls an "autonomous faculty," I wonder. In both meditation and privileged moments with language, knowledge is obtained that no intellectual undertaking can yield, and a new dimension of attention opens that goes beyond usual forms of consciousness.

Patchi pesters me with low sounds. It is time for our morning walk together. Descending the front stairs of the house with her, I notice enveloping planes of gray commanding the early dawn, falling in wide gradual sweeps, an atmosphere anesthetized by a motionless beam of daylight. While we walk, my mind relaxes as though it never wanted to think. Birdsong breaks on the flesh of my body and merges with my inner self, mysteriously protected from thought. There is a heightening of sensation, and I am immediately in a state of resonance—of something singing me. In my inner space, I simultaneously feel the morning star, the newspaper being delivered a block away, the elm tree at the creek, which I sense has been struck by lightning, and whatever links these objects.

Soon we pass the elm tree, which was indeed struck by lightning sometime during the night, now blackened and cleaved. Patchi enters the creek here for her daily swim. I am captivated by the similarity between this experience and the illumination in which Latin words of all sorts were mobile enough to cross space like a meteor shower. The more the silken web of my somatic-sensory system is impacted, the more expressive space seems to be as it penetrates the atoms of my body, uniting me with different planes of reality. There is limited understanding but immediate comprehension.

Arriving back home, I fail at my attempts to towel Patchi off as she displays her gargantuan will. I concede, moving us to the backyard, where she can wind-dry. While placing the grapevine clippings from days ago into waste containers for composting, I think about the elm tree by the creek and feel haunted by lightning's power, which has recently impacted my life immeasurably. Reflecting on Santi's lightning-struck sandals that were lovingly placed on the mountain peak shrouded in clouds, I'm reminded of philosopher Friedrich Nietzsche's words:

> He who with lightning-flash would touch
> Must long remain a cloud.[2]

I recall his consummate line:

> A lightning flash became my wisdom:
> With sword of adamant, it cloves me every
>   darkness.[3]

I wonder, might a lightning bolt be a supreme degree of speech, an exchange of mysteries for immediate comprehension?

While wandering into the house, I read more of Jephcott's text:

> Privileged moments tend to follow a
> characteristic pattern of development.
> They begin with heightened awareness....
> Consciousness then passes through
> progressive stages of intensification and
> unification, culminating in the ecstatic
> identification of the self with the world.
> In other words, there is an underlying
> continuum, a progression from a lower to
> higher state of development. The progressive
> heightening of awareness corresponds to the
> progressive expulsion of conceptual thought

from consciousness.... The continuum is latent in any of these moments. This does not mean, of course, that each one will necessarily pass through all the stages of the continuum, from the lowest to the highest level of intensity. But it implies that every privileged moment could do so, that the possibility of the full development exists in advance, as it were, of each particular experience, and also that the stages of this possible development are subject to a predetermined order.[4]

He continues:

There are of course many reasons why in practice this possibility might not be realized to its full extent. The most obvious reason is the natural tendency of the logical mind to re-assert its authority, to try to understand what is happening, and in so doing, to dispel the quality of experience it is attempting to grasp. Individual privileged moments may therefore be only fragmentary and partial realizations of the "ideal" continuum underlying the experience. But if allowed its full development, a privileged moment will necessarily follow the pattern established.[5]

I close the book tenderly, as if it were a holy text, thunderstruck by this apt description of a progression I have undergone during the illuminations. I know such a continuum underlies my experiences with privileged moments. Instead of an experience being scaled down to the measure of the individual body, the individual body expands to the measure of the experience. There is an inner immobility despite the motion within it, and then everything becomes luminous, limitless, and joyous. Even linear time disappears into the immobility—a state of consciousness that, free of any mental component, invites direct contact with things as they are. While you are in this state, a sensed object or idea isn't something you see or understand; it is something you are. Here it is possible to create without writing a word or painting a picture by simply allowing your inner life to be molded. While the progression of changes in my awareness as shaped by the illuminations likely began in the Andes during my time with Santi, I now sense I am being prepared for something yet to be born.

I feel graced by this discovery of an underlying continuum because it creates a semblance of order in my mind, but the satisfaction quickly fades. I have a gnawing awareness that the change underway, like a never weary wind, is affecting not only my identity but my perception of the meaning of everything around me. Part of me would gladly retain my old perceptual filter, which had me deriving the meaning of something by separating it from other things. But the glue of duality is dissolving, and something else is replacing it—an unsettling yet nourishing perception.

While handwashing dishes in the kitchen, I notice another apprehension bubbling up in me: workshops, keynote addresses, writing, and audio deadlines that require my attention. However, using my mind to conceptualize feels increasingly like trying to herd feral cats. My connection with concepts has gone barren. I wonder how this situation will play out. For now, I remain a cloud decidedly haunted by lightning.

9

Riding the Waves of Words
to Inner Worlds

Words seem to have a range and depth that,
unable to be predicted or controlled,
open us to augmented perception and ultimately
a fundamental sense of interconnectedness
with other realms.

WRITTEN CONTENT FOR THE LAST audio of a ten-part series, titled The Global Heart, is due by week's end. Because of my encounters with language illuminations, I barely trust my mind to create content like it used to. Since being by water often facilitates my writing when I have a deadline, I reschedule clients and leave in my Volkswagen Beetle for a four-day getaway to the north shore of Lake Superior. Patchi rides shotgun, her mostly white, tricolored coat glistening in the sun and emitting subtle bacterial odors from late-autumn creek swimming. She wears the aroma like a jeweled accessory.

While driving, I reflect on perhaps the most profound change I have undergone over the past year: no longer do I feel compelled to deal with my thoughts or tinker with my life circumstances, for the new dynamic at work within me is guiding me. All I must do is accept discoveries and let them flourish. This development makes it increasingly difficult for me to prepare written material. My mind is blank until I show up to give a lecture. After thirty years of preparing presentations, it is unsettling to trust that content will spontaneously appear in the moment, but somehow exactly what needs to be said arrives on cue. There seem to be fertile plains beyond time and space alive within me. Here, amidst the familiar silence and emptiness, phenomena seeking emergence germinate in black nitrogen-infused soil. It does not escape me that lightning produces nitrogen-rich earth.

I ponder the mystery of this inner richness, where one leaves behind observation, judgment, coveting. Impoverished thought generated by such habits of mind cannot abide in this space where the soul hears things the mind does not understand. I decide that illuminations may be earth's expressions moving through me, seeking visibility.

Cresting a hill on our approach to Lake Superior, I consider whether the inner richness discovered through the illuminations intimates the potential for a sustainable future. Does it reflect the shedding of ideas that have closed us down with false certainty, directed our attention away from the world, and filled us with only surface awareness, I ask myself. Certainly, this inner landscape shows that language impacts the ground of being, demanding profound receptivity and a return to the primordial silence from which words emerge, pulling us into an interrelatedness that is wholly enlivening.

Two and a half hours later Patchi and I arrive in Grand Marais and stop at a log cabin owned by an artist friend of Richard's, where I've been fortunate to enjoy solitude intermittently over the years. I survey the lake, with its ancient heartbeat of waves, a pulse that echoes through my veins, stitching me back into my own skin after the drive. Two stern cedar trees with roots descending through rock endure—silent, magnificent, reaching out with strong green branches, imbuing the air with fragrance—in symphony with the wind and water, including me in their composition.

The one-room cabin has the familiar feeling of home. Its freshly planed door and window casings exude a clean, airy look. The logs forming the walls are rough and weather-stained, while the rafters still have bark on them; the chimney, built of stones and sand from the shore, carries smoke outside efficiently, but only because of chinks between the cabin's boards. I can breathe fresh air without going outside. In fact, the cabin's room is not so much indoors as behind a door. Wind, birdsong, and the rustling of wildlife enter the interior, reminiscent of huts in the Andes that made me feel connected to the place and the people.

I bring in an armload of wood and build a fire in the stove. The damp logs hiss when the flame grabs them. Tree branches scrape against the windows as if trying to get in. Lake Superior, twenty feet away, is temperamental. Her mercurial nature arouses such reverence within me that for years I have affectionately called her Mother Superior. At times, she reveals powerful rip currents underneath her surface; other times she is lulled into the semblance of smooth glass. Lake Superior, arguably the deepest lake in the world, is a force to be reckoned with, never warmer than forty-two degrees Fahrenheit and known not to give up her dead, of which there are many. Today her turbulence resembles that of an eager dinner guest.

Hunkered down for the first three days, I mostly stare out the large window at the expanse of water and listen to the waves. Occasionally, Patchi and I walk aimlessly along the shore, where the fissured layers of waves crash rhythmically on the slip rock and, turning upon themselves, spatter clouds of spray.

By day four, I still have few words for the audio content. Sitting on a ladder-back chair at a table facing the lake, pen in hand, prepared to take dictation from the ebb and flow of the waves against the shore, I notice as 11:00 a.m. nears that I don't have a single sentence I haven't revised to death. I open the window, and a breeze wafts through, smelling of wet rock and cedar. The scent triggers an old, deep longing that seems to have no purpose. Then insistently words begin to rise in me like sap after winter, almost on cue with the sweet gum exuding from the dew on cabin timbers. My pen streams words in precipitous falls. The words begin diving, swimming, and floating, while undercurrents of silence and mystery beat in my pulse. My breath, throttled and sped up, is trapped in them. I ride the waves of these words to inner worlds as I write:

> The moment on the mountaintop was endless. Everything seemed to rise up in delight at the sound of avalanching snow cascading down nearby peaks. The rhythm lifted the earth. I could not feel my knees and was no longer occupying the narrow confines of my body; rather, I was an ascending force renewed to feed future life.

The words tumbling out leave a wake rippling through deep waters seemingly all the way back to the beginning of time. I know I am not their composer—merely their conduit—as this creation pours out of me then floats like a feather on water.

Complete, I stop, exhale, and stare at the lake. I'm reminded of the language illuminations set in the Middle East, during which I was suddenly inside language, no longer separate from it. Now language seems to gust through me, its sounds borne by the air that nourishes the landscape, like a loon's haunting liquid melody echoing the sounds of moving water.

I'm more convinced than ever that words are not merely an expression of the mind's content. Rather, I tell myself, they seem to have a range and depth that, unable to be predicted or controlled, open us to augmented perception and ultimately a sense of interconnectedness with other realms. In thinking about words' unique ability to give voice to the body's interactions with external reality, I'm reminded of the English poet David Whyte, who writes: "Human genius lies in the geography of the body and its conversation with the world."[1] He also notes:

> We might think of ourselves as each like a
> created geography, a confluence of inherited

flows.... It is the meeting place of our physical
body meeting all other bodies, corporeal and
elemental: a body breathed over by wind,
shaken by interior tremors and washed away
and rearranged by periodic floods; it has its
own hard-won language and its attempts
to order the un-orderable.... It intuits a
particular future for itself but is made in
conversation with all other futures.[2]

The human body's interactions with the world, as I
myself just discovered while gazing out the open window, can indeed be affected by sensory experiences.

Likewise, our sensory experiences can be
deeply influenced by our body's interactions with
the world. People listening to Beethoven's Eroica
symphony may not know of his talent for creating
music that impacts networks of intersecting ganglia in the human nervous system, causing facial
muscles to contract, likely even stimulating chemical
changes within us. Even so, listeners will feel their
breath quickening, their eyes weeping, their brains
engaging with images that spark new discoveries.
Language can do this too, I tell myself, in addition

to labeling external things. Surely, the power of words to activate somatic-sensory templates and unlock dimensions of interconnectedness has barely been realized, I conclude.

Not knowing whether I possess or am possessed by this linguistic endowment, with an insistent nudge from within I write:

> I hold out the cup of my spirit to ride
> the waves of words to inner worlds. Due
> to our habit of seeing language as a mere
> instrument of human expression, we—unable
> to receive what words are able to give—cannot
> conceive that we "have failed language."
> Perhaps in its own time language will show
> humanity its deeper dimensions, as I have
> been shown.

With my forehead pressed against the window, I perceive myself as a created geography at the confluence of everything around me, including the winter solstice air, the succulent plant on the table, Lake Superior's steel gray yet ever-changing appearance.

I walk along the shore one last time with Patchi before returning home. A soft feminine rain falls over us. Above it, sunlight filters through the few remaining leaves on the trees dotting the shoreline, seeming to let them know that new leaves, branches, and roots will one day come again. The leaves and the lake speak with the same voice, stirring the same songs in my depths. It is a voice that never silences.

Grateful to have finished writing the audio content and bewitched by these new insights into the power of words, I pack the car for the five-hour drive home. En route, I reflect on the myriad motions of words I observed echoing shifting elements of nature. And I see how in each instance, true to Jephcott's underlying continuum, the outer world seemed to manifest the qualities of my inner world, with feeling, consciousness, and knowledge becoming one. The landscape seemed to live, the elements of nature all participating, a dance normally concealed from human consciousness. I realize that I will never again confuse a verb that rolls with one that floats or spins, having experienced the difference in my body. I then have a more penetrating insight: being a mouthpiece for language is not a sudden burst of manifestation but an organic unfolding of new growth, just as trees in spring receive new leaves, branches, and roots.

10

Holy Word Power

*Listening can catalyze a transformation
from perceiving as a separate self
to perceiving as part of a current
connecting all things.*

EARLY THIS MORNING, during the hours of vigil when whatever has something to say speaks, I awaken from a lucid dream. Hoping its content might assist me in recording the narrative for the last audio in the series, I grab my journal from the nightstand and make an entry:

11 January 2014 ~ 6:40 a.m.: Awaken within a dream. I'm inside the body of a dolphin, adept at using its sonar language system and swimming as a member of the pod.

The ocean is unceasingly astir, yet there is
no problem with navigation. My dolphin
body seems fashioned by waves. The great
bodies of our pod are polished like weapons—
our snouts nearly flattened by the mass
water that withstands our progress, our
fins as rigid and cutting as iron, though
sensitive to our sonar signals—being
steered toward their destinations. No matter
the properties of the wind and water, the
uncertainties of sea floors, the circulation of
warm currents and immiscible streams, we
are mysteriously confident between channels
of treacherous estuaries.

I feel beyond creation, inside the creator.
There is great buoyancy, a shimmering
aliveness that is both still and moving. My
undulating body is universal, with no central
I in charge. The other dolphins, the fish,
the coral, the sky and sun play like a chord
through the body. We navigate through
echolocation, emitting clicking sounds
that bounce off each nearby object and
back to us through the seawater, letting

us know its location. Matter and sensation are connected. Sight has become metaphysical touch.

As I finish penning the entry at 7:30 a.m., Princess yowls for her morning treats and Patchi stares at me as though I will never feed her. I remain altered, still experiencing sound and tactile vision forming a complex system and buoyancy greater than gravity. After steeping a cup of green tea, I plop down in my living room rocking chair. Princess comes to sit on my lap, moving with a feathery, unfurling gait before assuming the regal posture of a jaguar. Her purring becomes symphonic as I slowly finger her sleek coat. It is a beautiful moment, simple in its immediacy. The surround sound of her purring soon envelops me like an aura of light—the sign of an approaching illumination.

I feel my breath slowing and the atmosphere becoming still. I am now guided below my surface breath to the silent, invisible breath flowing like a current through all of life, connecting forests with desert landscapes. A sensation of boundlessness arises in my body. I then hear:

Bathe deeply in the current of sound
vibrating within you, permeating your body
and everything around it simultaneously.
Let yourself be absorbed into its vastness,
as if into the song of a brightly shining
constellation. The pulsating emptiness
you are coming to know is the source
of all things.

Now, as if hearing them emerge from
this source within you, listen to the following
vowel sounds:

Ahhh
  Eeee
    Oooo
      Ommm
        Humm.

Savor the sounds, inhabit their subtle,
ever-changing tones, layer upon layer,
letting yourself be deeply touched by
them as they come alive within you.
Then observe where the sounds go as
they wane.

I hear a hum, as if a string has been plucked inside me. Then I feel an inner vibration throughout my entire body, much like the tactile vision in this morning's dream. Oneness has seized me.

As the illumination fades, my inner vibration quiets, and I am suffused with peace. Gazing out the window at the landscape, I am stunned by the human body's enormous capacity for sensation. Just as deserts are devoid of fertile soil because water has never reached them, I tell myself, spaces in the human body that were never touched by sensation are likewise devoid of fertility yet indeed have the potential for growth under more favorable conditions.

Feeling sonar-like sensations arising within me, I set up the audio equipment on my office desk and gather as much presence as possible. Closing my eyes, I feel my pulse slow and I am soon inside the current of sound. I press the Record button and begin to speak the words coming alive within me and finding their way to my lips. My breath crescendos, then softens. My pace accelerates, then slows. As I submit to the silence around each sound charging through me, the words, as if activated by the silence, come forth pungent with meaning. My body, too, feels enlivened as I listen to them.

Complete, I press Stop and look up. I am astonished to realize that words can catalyze a transformation from perceiving as a separate self to perceiving as part of a current connecting all things. I wonder if the directive to enter the current of sound was actually summoning me to listen to the voice of source soaked in the silences.

Around 7:00 p.m., I call my friend Michael, a personal assistant to the Hindu sage Maharishi Mahesh Yogi during the Transcendental Meditation movement of the 1970s, eager to share the morning's illuminations with someone long familiar with mystical experiences. After a quick catch-up, I describe the two events. He then laughs heartily and says, "Brahmarishi Devarat, a disciple of Ramana Maharshi, once gave us a four-hour lecture on the gap between syllables of the first word of the fire god Agni in the Rig-Veda. In the gap, he explained, is the totality of everything and everything not." Having experienced the space between

vowel sounds this morning and in prior illuminations, I understand his comment.

Near the end of our conversation, I ask, "Do you know of anyone who has had persistent mystical experiences that seemed to have come from an invisible hand with a governing aim?"

After a long silence, he replies, "Eventually someone in history will come to mind. Meanwhile, I am going to send you an MP3 audio file of Maharishi giving a lecture on Vedic grammar. Your experiences remind me of that lecture." We end our conversation with my agreeing to visit him in Utah in October and deliver a talk to his local meditation community.

I promptly download the audio file and listen to the seventeen-minute lecture. Within the first minute, I react viscerally to Maharishi's words, my breath mysteriously deep, as if the distance it travels is boundless. Maharishi, in an informal, relaxed manner, says:

> Grammar teaches not only the relationship
> and mutual coordination of different words.
> Grammar uncovers the reality contained

in each word. What is a word? This is a
word which at its core has eternal, infinite,
unbounded being....[1]

He continues:

> Meaning tells the whole story on the level
> of understanding. Sound tells the whole
> story on the level of experience. What is
> to be unfolded to knowledge and experience
> through the word is that which lies beyond
> the obvious. That which lies beyond the
> obvious must be experienced to be known.
> Experience ends in opening the awareness
> to the unboundedness.... Unless that
> unboundedness is experienced, language
> has lost its true value. Something will
> be gained, something will be gained,
> something will be gained, but not the
> totality which is contained in every word....
> At the deeper levels there will be more
> connectedness, more connectedness until
> it reaches the ultimate connectedness. Inert,
> now it is lively.[2]

I'm reminded of aspects of this morning's illuminations on sound—the experience of connectedness with the dolphins and of boundlessness, like the songs of constellations.

Finally, Maharishi imparts:

> If one knows how to use a word, then one would use any level of the word, gross or finer, more subtle or subtlest, celestial or transcendent. Transcendent use of the word would be in the fullness of Brahman (full awareness), where the wholeness of creation could be influenced or comprehended or activated by that one awareness.[3]

Maharishi's view of the transcendent use of words strikes a chord in me. That a word could conceivably influence "the wholeness of creation" awakens me to the unfathomable power of words. I dub this phenomenon "holy word power" and infer that such power explains why when Gandhi sat in spoken prayer the fighting in India stopped and why high-ranking Q'ero medicine men in ceremony can call in dry lightning strikes on a mountaintop. Ultimately, the power of any word depends on the mindset of the person using it and the depth of embodied awareness from which it rises, I conclude. Reminding myself that the power of words effects changes when they are listened to as well as read, I flash on this morning's dream, where the uncertainties of sea floors were easily traversed as we navigated with sonar, absorbed in the vastness of the current of sound vibrating within. I recall how the gap between vowel sounds, or even between the syllables of a spoken word, produces a similar vibration in the body, leading to an experience of boundlessness.

Weary from the day, I look out at the rising crescent moon and feel its translucent flesh transporting my earthly body. Mixed with its pull are the mysterious voices of the wind, the treetops, the clouds, the stars. I make use of this exalted moment to allow my spirit to rise aloft. Soaring, I apprehend how expanded states of awareness prompted by language reveal a web of relations in which human beings are included because holy word power has woven us into it.

11

The Hidden Motion of Language

In a moment occasioned by language,
a profound forwarding within the somatic-sensory
system had thrust open an interior trapdoor
to unbound awareness.

WINTER HAS ARRIVED in full regalia. This morning it is thirty-two degrees below zero, and snow falls lightly. Patchi lives for walks in these temperatures that seem to free her otherwise encumbered primal arctic spirit.

Intending to stroll outside with her, I quickly prepare. In the Andes, I learned not to separate myself from the elements. The Q'ero wear open-toe sandals and require few layers of clothing, even when temperatures plummet below zero. The ancient rhythms of the earth have so insinuated themselves into the hearts of the villagers that it would never occur to them to seek protection from the elements. To the contrary, they see themselves as organs of the earth; indeed, the word for human being in Quechua is *runa*, which translates to animated earth. For me, however, some winter gear is still required in these temperatures.

Once Patchi and I are out walking in the winter light, there arises from a coiled stillness within me a sensation that can only be described as a profound forwarding. It is like breaking out in goose bumps inside the body then feeling the momentum build until inside and outside become one, animating a wordless conversation that seems to unite cosmos, earth, and human being. Energized by the rays of winter light as they flash from every direction, I feel the space around and within me vibrating with musical undertones that simultaneously pierce the senses from without and undulate within.

As I continue to walk, with snow crunching under my boots, I ponder Rilke's revelatory intuition about the motion of music:

Music is almost like the air of higher regions:
we breathe it deeply into the lungs of our

spirit, and it infuses a more expansive blood into our hidden circulation. Yet *how far* music reaches beyond us! Yet, *how far* it pushes on with no regard for us! Yet, how much of which it carries right through us we still fail to seize! Alas, we fail to seize it, alas, we lose it.[1]

I wonder whether language, like music, mobilizes what Rilke calls our "hidden circulation," making it capable of invigorating a feeling of unity between realms. I wonder, too, if language is a medium that, through a profound forwarding, can liberate individuals from focusing solely on surface matters to seizing more of what language has to offer. I remind myself that language made my body, previously deadened, come alive again and feel unified with nature—all the more reason to allow language to reach beyond our thinking minds, estranged as they are from the intelligence of our sensing bodies and the gift of their "hidden circulation." Perhaps the thinking mind is akin to an outer layer of clothing, insulating but ultimately not needed, I conclude.

After we return home, I eat a breakfast of dolmas, cottage cheese, toast with humus, and a cup of green tea, then drive to my office to see clients. My first, Ariel, is a twenty-year-old Olympic gymnast hopeful, referred by her sports medicine physician due to a traumatic brain injury for which she is taking a gap year in college. After several months of sessions, she is ready to return to college and has decided to retire from gymnastics.

Ariel sits on the couch across from me. She removes her winter boots and, while peeling off three layers of outerwear, finishes a text to her mother, a scientist who works in Beijing. Ariel flashes a giant grin and announces, "I'm going to visit my mom for a month before returning to school." She looks ready to meet the world again.

I smile and ask, "Do you remember the first thing you said to me when we met?"

"I am so fucking depressed," she says. She emphasizes the *f* in *fucking*, almost giddy to be saying the expletive aloud.

I've sat with Ariel through brain fog, headaches, nausea, light sensitivity, grief over retiring from a sport that defined her life, and the ending of her relationship with a boyfriend because, in her words, "he doesn't understand that *love* is a verb."

During our conversations, I have listened, gently guided, and occasionally cajoled to help her unveil the next steps in life. I'm aware that sadness is sometimes an expression of the paralysis we experience while alone with an unfamiliar future that has begun to transform us and, shifting the ground under our feet, caused us to feel momentarily abandoned by our former reality. My objective has been to provide a space where her future presents a ground for her feet to eagerly explore.

Near the end of what is likely our last session, I ask, "Do you feel mentally ready to go through final exams again?" Ariel is wicked smart. Her father is a physicist, her mother a chemist. She, too, would like to become a chemist.

She replies, "I am not sure, since I've never really studied for one. I'm going to say something I've never told anyone because it makes me sound crazy. When I take a multiple-choice test, something weird happens: I read the choices and can always find the right answer because its sound is harmonious with the sound of the question."

I ask, "What about exams that require written responses?"

She responds, "Essentially it is the same. I know when what I am writing is harmonious with the question because of the sound." She places her hand inches from her heart and rotates it in a circular motion.

I am captivated, noting how a motion propelling the sounds of language gives her access to knowing.

She runs her hands through her hair and quickly pulls it back into a ponytail. Now looking like a fourteen-year-old, she asks, "Does that seem weird to you? It's not like I'm hearing voices or anything."

"Is it like a current of sound, and can you feel it in your body?" I ask.

She becomes wide-eyed and replies, "Yes, have you ever heard of such a thing?" Nonchalantly, I say, "I know what you mean. Gleaning knowledge through sound in motion is a sensory gift. I bet it will be there when the time comes to take your exams." As she slips her boots and winter garments back on and we hug good-bye, I am aware that underneath the layers of cold weather gear is a young woman facing the world ahead with unbridled awareness.

After her departure, I water a soon-to-bloom orchid oddly burgeoning forth in my office in the dead of winter, marveling at how nature awakens us to significant events quietly and unobtrusively, as if we might otherwise deem ourselves crazy. I am elated as I contemplate the likelihood of a proliferation of similar instances of profound forwarding slipping into human interactions virtually unnoticed.

My next client, Maria, is an East Indian surgeon in her mid-fifties, a longtime meditator whose only daughter was recently killed in an automobile accident. She enters my office quietly, disturbs nothing, not even the air, as she slips off her boots, removes her coat, and sits cross-legged on the sofa, beside the folded blanket I keep there. She then announces, "Well, it's official. My husband is having an extramarital affair, and I leave tomorrow to deliver a talk in India."

It is our third session together, and I've yet to witness her grief, only a lifestyle that keeps her moving most of the time. I want Maria to feel comfortable in consultation but not so comfortable that I am not helping her. Sometimes a loving truth bomb is needed.

I hand her a cup of hot water, something she requested during our previous two sessions, sit down in my chair, and remark, "Your daughter's death had to have been difficult for your husband. I wonder if he stepped out of your marriage to seek emotional support?" I let my statement linger, knowing that honesty is stronger medicine than sympathy, which may console but often conceals.

She shifts her position, covering herself with the blanket. Her voice falters for a second, then she says, "I love my husband. I will not leave him, but he will need to end his affair."

A long silence ensues. Bolstered by the natural ease between us, I say, "I wonder how you and your husband might share a moment feeling the loss of your daughter."

She closes her eyes. A bright luminosity instantly floods the room. A moment later I hear an inner sound—a soft rustling at first then a crescendo of ticking, drumming, hissing, crackling, and finally a roar of alarming intensity. I am stunned not so much by the mysterious power of the words spoken as by the movement they mobilized. It's as though the initial rush of sound was joined by other sounds, enhancing the resulting volume till the cosmos had joined our session.

Maria opens her mouth to speak, but I am deaf to everything except the sounds now humming throughout my body. I am reminded of what physicist Fritjof Capra once said when comparing the nature of reality to music:

> The nature of reality is much closer to music than to a machine.... The essence of a melody does not live in its notes; it lies in the relationships between the notes, in the intervals, frequencies, and rhythms. When a string is set vibrating, we hear not only a single tone but also its overtones—an entire scale is sounded. Thus, each note involves all the others, just as each subatomic particle involves all others.[2]

When the sounds subside, Maria begins silently weeping. Several minutes go by before she whispers: "What just happened, Christina? I felt my daughter's presence for the first time since she passed. She was radiant and happy." Maria then stands up, placing her delicate surgeon hands, right over left, on her heart, and continues to weep silently, swaying back and forth as if listening to music.

I'm relieved to have emerged from the invisible human interaction with some mutual understanding that something of great significance had entered the session. There is no map for such terrain. The atmosphere between two people in communication takes on a life of its own; though both influence its motion, neither one controls it. Silently, I stand up, close my eyes, and, pulsating from head to toe, sway back and forth with Maria for several minutes, knowing that movement gives expression to buried emotion in a way that speech sometimes cannot, leading to greater awareness.

Maria then says, "I'm canceling my trip to India. I have amends to make in my marriage, which I have all but ignored. It is time to come to terms with how my life has changed." I make a mental note that intimacy with her husband may be intertwined with the shared loss of their daughter.

I nod in agreement. Maria, feeling complete, prepares to depart five minutes early, saying, "I don't know what happens in here, but I always leave feeling changed in some way."

Holding her coat out for her to slip into, I flash on Capra's insight about the vibratory impact of even a single sound—why so much as the pluck of a violin string or the utterance of a word can cause the listener to hear a cacophony of sounds and why every atom of my body now appeared to be vibrating. Finally, I reply, "That's okay. I never know what is going to happen in here either."

Remarkably, in a moment occasioned by language, a profound forwarding within the somatic-sensory system had thrust open an interior trapdoor to an unbound awareness. And immediately the eternal incarnated in time, sweeping us into its flow. No longer were Maria and I separated from the eternal.

In reflecting on my meetings with both clients today, I realize that I tapped in to this hidden dimension of language, the movement propelling it, and its motion inside us. I now see that when we objectify language we relate to its outer layer, its "winter coat," but when we surrender to the power of words and sense its movement within us, we awaken to its many gifts. Now, language is living.

While preparing to leave my office, I watch the arctic wind gusting outside. It seems to blow wherever it pleases and, while I hear its sound, I cannot tell where it is coming from or where it is going. How similar the hidden motion of language is to the wind, I tell myself, and likely all other forces born of spirit.

12

Stewardship of Living Language

*The changes in consciousness occasioned
by language that first appear in a few people
will, through their spoken and written words,
gradually appear in others.*

SITTING ON MY DECK in a rocking chair, wrapped in a light fleece blanket, I am spellbound by the night. A warm wind stirs, like a gentle gardener's hand touching budding roses, releasing their fragrance under a duvet of moonlight. Then the darkness envelops me like a womb. My body feels weightless in every extremity. Swaddled in peacefulness, I plunge into sleep. From deep down in the primal clay of my flesh there soon comes a thin, continuous noise; then an unnatural light floods my being. An illumination unfolds on the stewardship of living language. When it is complete, I rise, the cavernous night penetrating my skin like a corrosive salt. I wander inside, steep a cup of chamomile tea, and pull out my journal to record the highlights of this illumination before it fades:

June 2015: Stewardship of Living Language

- Language—vocabulary, syntax, pronunciation, and intonation—is always changing. A steward of living language contributes to this development by broadening language's capacity to express wide-ranging and subtle gradations of feeling and perception.

- A steward of living language feels socially obligated to respond to changes in language, to further its potential to increase consciousness and to battle against its degradation.

- It matters little whether a steward of living language has a large audience in their lifetime. Cultural developments take root not by inseminating an entire population but by "seeding" a few of its citizens, a vanguard of individuals ready to assimilate innovation.

- The changes in consciousness occasioned by language that take root in those people will, through their spoken and written words, gradually appear in others over successive generations.

- The changes in consciousness that take place in a steward of living language will soon activate additional changes in their consciousness.

Setting my pen down, I reflect on individuals of long ago whose words live on in scripture—the holy ones, perhaps the illuminated ones. The current power of their spoken and written words, I am convinced, derives from the depths at which they were sown. Just as long-living trees have the deepest roots, so do long-living verses, their root systems shrouded in the eternal. Similarly, the effect of their words as they come to light springs from the ancient speaker or writer's expanse of consciousness.

Still lost in reverie, I think of how these writers and speakers, all stewards of living language, had accessed within themselves a sense of the sublime and an awareness of their unity with all of creation because they had reclaimed their capacity to feel. In effect, they had awakened within themselves an ability to enter the motion underlying their somatic-sensory perceptions—to see through surface features and feel the forces underneath them. Wearied from the illumination and reflections, I retire for the night, sliding between the sheets after a short battle with Princess, who eventually agrees to share the undercover terrain.

At 11:00 a.m. the next day, an airport taxi is waiting to take Sheri and me to a flight to Missouri, where I am to give a keynote address at the International Society for the Study of Subtle Energies and Energy Medicine Conference. On the plane, Sheri goes over the conference itinerary with me.

After landing at St. Louis Airport, we join a volunteer from the conference who is waiting to chauffeur us to Unity Village, world headquarters for the Unity Church, where the event is to be held. On our way there, the driver tells Sheri the names of the speakers who will present over the next few days, while I watch the scenery outside my window, candescent shades of green everywhere on the spacious hills of pastureland. Upon arrival at Unity Village, the driver gives Sheri name tags, food passes, and plastic folders, then drops us off at our room.

We spend the afternoon wandering on foot through the serene, wooded acres dotted with Mediterranean architecture, meandering through award-winning rose gardens, and strolling over brick bridges between fountains misting with rose fragrance in the heat of the day. When the time approaches to give my keynote address, I enter the light-infused auditorium with its theater-style seating to do a quick sound check; the acoustics of the space bellow sound pristinely. Once the auditorium fills and the lights dim, my friend and colleague Deborah introduces me, adding, "I know

Dr. Donnell well enough to announce there will be no PowerPoint presentation. Having listened to many of her talks, I suggest closing your eyes as you take in what she imparts today."

I head up the stairs to the stage and stand behind the podium. I take a deep breath, welcome the six hundred people in attendance, pause long enough to notice discomfort, then recite the title of my forty-minute speech: "Tending Our Evolving Consciousness." My circulation slows, my breath deepens. I begin: "What does it mean to be human?"

There is a long pause as I make eye contact with the audience, then say: "Are we a wish to be fulfilled? Are we a question to be resolved? Are we designed for more eventualities than we can know?"

After another long pause, my breath and body touch the current of silence. I repeat: "What does it mean to be human?"

There is an acceleration, and now my breath is throttled, invigorated, slowed down. I continue: "Can we expect this body, our current means of manifestation on earth, to be able to change progressively into something capable of expressing a greater reality? Can we endow it with a receptivity to words spoken or printed, in which we instantly reach the stars, eliminating time and distance, as if everything were taking place within us? If I thought otherwise, I would not be standing here before you."

Paradoxically, I feel the presence within me and around me of a strong, silent current of incredible beauty, aimless yet nourishing, like a meandering river. I continue speaking for thirty-five minutes and conclude the presentation with the same four questions with which it began.

The audience remains dead silent. I'm relieved because I can still feel the current undulating in the room and wonder if some members of the audience sense it.

Moments later people begin lining up at the microphone for a question-and-answer session. Many comment that they have little recollection of the talk but describe an altered state of consciousness they experienced while listening to it. I am surprised by their reports and imagine that they are, too. In thirty minutes, I answer only two questions; the remaining time is taken up with remarks from people who were transported to unfamiliar dimensions during the talk.

Three days later, Sheri and I, unaccustomed to the bustle of conferences, eagerly prepare to leave. Sheri is tired of running interference for me with people who want to engage me in conversation. For me, the distillation of so much thought mars the stillness of my mind, and only with a still mind can I feel the presence of mysterious forces in my midst.

On the short flight home, I reflect on the audience's comments about being so transported they had no recollection of the content delivered—an often-occurring situation. Many of my longtime students can listen to an audio, then three days later listen again and swear they never heard it before. Last year, during a book signing following a talk I gave in Seattle, a woman thanked me for recommending a title on Australian Aborigines. Thinking I had lost my mind, I asked Sheri, sitting beside me, "Did I recommend a book during that talk?" Sheri replied, "I didn't hear you refer to a book." The woman later sent an email thanking me again for the recommendation, noting it was the right book at the right time. In reply, I told her I never

recommended a book and my assistant corrobo-
rated this. She answered, "How odd, because the
woman next to me heard it too, and wrote it down."

Mystified by such occurrences, I wonder
whether the sounds of words in the talks I present are perhaps eclipsed by the invisible currents
entering the room, like those I felt at Unity Village.
Could it be that a profound forwarding of words
spoken at the Unity Village address and at my talk
in Seattle had, for some listeners, thrust open an
interior trapdoor to unbound awareness? And if
so, I reasoned, might these listeners be among the
vanguard of people ready to assimilate innovation?

When I arrive home, Patchi greets me at the door
as if I were a long lost pack member, while Princess rebuffs my approaches. Abby has left a lovely
bouquet of freshly picked pink peonies on the fireplace mantel and, on the dining room table, a box
containing a magnificent display of delicate baclava
nestled amidst a profusion of deep chartreuse tissue
paper. Too tired to enjoy these treasures, I repair to
my bedroom.

The next morning I feel something akin to a hangover, a sensation I often experience after an extended time teaching. Finally, at 2:00 p.m. I make my way to the grocery store as the refrigerator is empty. Quickly finding the items on my list, I stand at the checkout counter behind a mother unloading a full grocery cart of provisions onto the conveyor belt while managing two children between the ages of three and five, their little hands everywhere. When she attempts to pay the cashier, none of her debit cards works. Fifteen minutes pass. I can see there is a language barrier between the two. Distressed, the woman looks furtively toward me, inky black eyebrows gracing her broad forehead.

In a flash, I see an elderly woman with the same inky black eyebrows sitting in a wheelchair in a small house. I assume it is her mother and they live as a multigenerational family, which would explain the adult Depends on the conveyor belt. A little kindness is in order. I say to the cashier, "Would you be kind enough to bag her groceries? I will pay for them." He complies. I take my credit card out and gesture to the woman that I will pay. She bursts into tears while chasing her youngest child.

After paying for the items in my cart as well, I exit the store to find the woman in the parking lot still loading groceries into her car. She gives me a warm hug with effusive thank-yous in broken English.

While driving home, I reflect on how extremely sensitive I've become to sensory input and how steeped I am in a feeling of communion with all, as if some boundary between myself and external reality has dissolved. My sense of direct knowing in the grocery store, like similar liminal experiences I now have without the light and language cues that accompanied earlier messages from the invisible world, was no doubt shaped by, and likely an outgrowth of, my years of language illuminations. In these moments of knowing, I initially feel myself becoming a conduit for vibrations more ancient than human existence. Then my awareness undergoes a metamorphosis, altering how I see myself and the world around me.

Once home, I unload the week's sustenance. After making a cup of green tea, I sit down at the dining room table with the gift box of pastries, nibbling on baclava and drinking scalding tea in small sips. I review my notes on the stewardship of living language and contemplate the restorative perspectives such individuals can bring to today's world. Experiencing the breadth of expanded states of awareness that result from tuning in to living language, they can advocate for diminishing the role of the controlling mind in human interactions. Able to experience a word emerging from stillness and, behind it, a wake rippling through waters leading back to the beginning of time, they can also commend the virtues of stillness, within which, they know, lies a primordial power. I conclude that stewards of living language, simply by embodying an experience of this primordial power and the interconnectedness of humanity and indeed all of life, have much to contribute to our present-day world while transporting us to a new consciousness.

Following a final sip of tea, I realize that stewardship of living language may ultimately demonstrate a gradual transition in human evolution, signs of which already appear in some of the new human capacities now emerging. I have an inkling that millennia ago, flight might have begun altering the functioning of early pterosaurs' bodies before these reptiles became flying vertebrates. And I suspect that one and a half million years ago early hominids might have experienced new vibrations stirring in their brains, heralding the emergence of language. I cannot help but marvel: Are *Homo sapiens* perhaps on the threshold of someday becoming *Homo illuminous*?

Conclusion

Human consciousness advances not linearly but in unforeseen leaps—in revelatory epiphanies experienced one person at a time, often quietly, in the margins of life. We can imagine how, amidst flickering light aglow in dark caves, early *Homo erectus* acted instinctively, with inner and outer somatic-sensory impressions so unified that thought had no place. Later, during a period of dramatic climate change, new cognitive structures emerged, making way for *Homo sapiens'* problem-solving abilities and language skills. As a result of these developments, we *Homo sapiens* now think before acting.

My encounters with living language have shown me that these evolutionary advances, while helpful for survival amidst environmental instability, may have obstructed humans from accessing their ancestral somatic-sensory system—and, with it, their receptivity to intuitive insights and their sense of connectedness to all of life. I have also learned that the opening of this trapdoor through an experience with living language, can propel a sudden leap forward in consciousness, reinvigorating our sense of oneness with each other and the surrounding world. Perhaps such an integration is now occurring, an advance in human consciousness sparked by *today's* need for survival amidst environmental instability—a new expression of language as an evolutionary medium.

Indeed, beneath words lie mysteries. Maharishi, whom I consider a steward of living language, states:

> What is to be unfolded to knowledge and
> experience through the word is that which
> lies beyond the obvious. That which lies
> beyond the obvious must be experienced
> to be known. Experience ends in opening
> the awareness to the unboundedness.
> At the deeper levels there will be more
> connectedness, more connectedness until
> it reaches the ultimate connectedness.
> Inert, now it is lively.[1]

In experiencing how language not only represents worldly phenomena but also deepens our sense of connection to the whole of creation, we can let the natural motion of its mysterious tributaries lead us to the ocean of origins.

In this era of global upheaval—with its pandemic, wars, political unrest, systemic racism, and climate change—when searching for external solutions to problems often seems to underscore disunity between people, as well as between people and the earth, language may in fact be inviting us to surrender to its unifying potential. In surrendering, after all, we experience a wider cosmic net of relationships, furthering both our growth in unified consciousness and our collective earthly survival.

My experiences during illuminations point to an expansive web of relations into which language has woven us. The discovery of them can touch the innermost nexus of our existence and lead to an understanding that all is one. Those who access this secret place where primordial power nurtures all of existence, inevitably add more spirit to the perceived world and aid in awakening humanity to its connection to the whole. May we humans come to comprehend the deeper function of living language: its holy power and role in our evolving consciousness and collective earthly survival.

Notes

Chapter 4

1. E. F. N. Jephcott, *Proust and Rilke: The Literature of Expanded Consciousness* (New York: Harper and Row, 1972), 17–26. Descriptions of "privileged moments" experienced by various authors, as reported by E. F. N. Jephcott, include the following: Valéry, "Everything suddenly ceases to have its ordinary effect, and what we guide ourselves by tends to vanish"; Baudelaire, "Things seem to shine more and more brightly in an ever-growing light" and "Sounds have a musical timbre"; Flaubert, "The sky seemed to be expanding and the whole face of nature changing....an inexpressible comprehension of the unrevealed wholeness of things"; Poulet, "Time can be felt passing like a breeze.....the sense of an absolute homogeneity between the different elements composing the moment"; Roquentin, "Flood of divine feeling."

2. Rainer Maria Rilke, *The Notebooks of Malte Laurids Brigge* (New York: Penguin, 2009), in Jephcott, Proust and Rilke, 155.

3. Ibid., 161–162.

Chapter 5

1. T. S. Eliot, in David Steindl-Rast and Sharon Lebell, *Music of Silence: A Sacred Journey through the Hours of the Day* (Berkeley, CA: Seastone, 2002), 11.

Chapter 6

1. Hazrat Inayat Kahn, *The Music of Life: The Inner Nature and Effects of Sound* (New Lebanon, NY: Omega Publications, 2005), 178.

2. Joachim Ernst-Berendt, *The World Is Sound: Nada Brahma—Music and the Landscape of Consciousness* (Rochester, VT: Destiny Books, 1983), 172.

3. Rainer Rilke, *The Notebooks of Malte Laurids Brigge* (New York: Penguin, 2009), in Jephcott, Proust and Rilke, 161.

4. Ibid.

Chapter 7

1. T. S. Eliot, *On Poetry and Poets* (Boston: Faber and Faber, 1957), 24.

Chapter 8

1. Jephcott, *Proust and Rilke*, 21, 29.

2. Friedrich Nietzsche, in Gaston Bachelard, *Air and Dreams: An Essay on the Imagination of Movement* (Dallas, TX: Dallas Institute Publications, 1988), 133.

3. Ibid.

4. Jephcott, *Proust and Rilke*, 30.

5. Ibid.

Chapter 9

1. David Whyte, *Consolations: The Solace, Nourishment, and Underlying Meaning of Everyday Words* (Langley, WA: Many Rivers Press, 2015), 78–79.

2. Ibid.

Chapter 10

1. Maharishi Mahesh Yogi, "Vedic Grammar," audio talk from a private collection, 1972.

2. Ibid.

3. Ibid.

Chapter 11

1. Ulrich Baer, *The Poet's Guide to Life: The Wisdom of Rilke* (New York: The Modern Library, 2005), 143.

2. Johannes Kepler, in Ernst-Berendt, *The World Is Sound*, xii.

Conclusion

1. Yogi, "Vedic Grammar."

Suggested Reading

Abram, David. *The Spell of the Sensuous: Perception and Language in a More-Than-Human World.* New York: Vintage Books, 1977.

Buhner, Stephen Harrod. *Ensouling Language: On the Art of Nonfiction and the Writer's Life.* Rochester, VT: Inner Traditions, 2010.

Dowrick, Stephanie. *In The Company of Rilke: Why a 20th-Century Visionary Poet Speaks So Eloquently to 21st-Century Readers.* New York: Jeremy P. Tarcher/Penguin, 2011.

Ernst-Berendt. *The World Is Sound: Music and the Landscape of Consciousness.* Rochester, VT: Destiny Books, 1983.

Jephcott, E. F. N. *Proust & Rilke: The Literature of Expanded Consciousness.* New York: Harper & Row, 1972.

Khan, Hazrat Inayat. *The Music of Life: The Inner Nature and Effects of Sound.* New Lebanon, NY: Omega Publications, 2005.

Picard, Max. *The World of Silence.* Wichita, KS: Eighth Day Press, 2002.

Sardello, Robert. Silence: *The Mystery of Wholeness.* Berkeley, CA: North Atlantic Books, 2008.

Williams, Duane. *Language And Being: Heidegger's Linguistics.* New York: Bloomsbury, 2017.

Acknowledgments

Producing a book reminds me of wine making. Both endeavors strive to bring forth a living body in which many diverse spirits are nurtured and kept in balance.

In making wine, the vine, by heaping up debris, composes its own soil, which it feeds its fruits. I owe deep gratitude to Suzanne Savage, Deborah Goldberg, Michael Speight, Mary Jo Peppler, Barbara Arney, Louise Dollin, Katharine Weiser, Sue Steindorf, Catharine Campaign, and Richard Russo, who read draft chapters of this book and offered guidance about its foundational "soil composition." I also thank Alicia Bauers for the astute attention given to nuance in the Spanish translations, which contributed to its health.

In wine making, the vine alchemically harmonizes elements of the earth, giving the wine its "must density." I am deeply grateful to Sheri Harris and Lynn Powers for their insightful and meticulous reading of the book at various stages, lending crucial ongoing help and support so the book could at this point achieve its proper must density.

The changing of the seasons over time allows wine to properly age. I wish to express enduring thanks to my dear friend, writing partner, and fellow writer Julianne Cohen. She was the first to hear the manuscript speak, and her well-tuned ear, keen editorial eye, and compassionate guidance on narrative, tone, and structure helped the book "age" in a way that enhanced its character.

On occasion, a comet passing overhead makes for a special vintage of wine, its long tail of celestial liquid, distilled in the firmament, adding subtle, inspired substance. My editor, Ellen Kleiner, is the comet who graced the writing of this book, archiving the language illuminations, tending to the growth of the vine, and overseeing the book's aging process. Over sixteen years, she has taught me how to be a writer and an author. My gratitude for her is boundless.

About the Author

Christina Donnell, PhD—a clinical psychologist, author, and spiritual teacher—is the director of the Winds of Change Association, a Minneapolis-based educational organization dedicated to offering programs that tend humankind's evolving consciousness. She is also the author of the multiple award–winning book *Transcendent Dreaming: Stepping into Our Human Potential,* a foray into the quantum nature of the human body. She maintains a consultation practice, teaches, and speaks worldwide, her lyrical prose, infused with transmissions of the unseen, captivating audiences of all ages. For more information, visit www.christinadonnell.com.